ID667548

YIN

YANG

YOU

YIN YANG YOU

Biohacking With Ancient Codes

ANLONG XU, PHD

&

MEHMET OZ, MD

with **Rob Sinnott, PhD, Jeremy Tian, MD, PhD, Lepeng Wang, PhD, Ted Spiker**

Illustrations by Nadia Chen

YIN YANG YOU: BIOHACKING WITH ANCIENT CODES

Copyright © 2021 Anlong Xu, Ph.D., President Beijing University of Chinese Medicine and Mehmet C. Oz, M.D., Columbia University.

ISBN 978-1-7372985-0-2 (hardcover)
ISBN 978-1-7372985-1-9 (ebook)

Printed in the United States of America

10 9 8 7 6 5 4 3 2 1

Illustrated by Nadia Chen
Book design by Morgan Crockett | Firewire Creative
Printed by Book Printers of Utah

yinyangyou.com

DEDICATED TO ALL THOSE SEEKING
HEALTH FROM THE TRADITIONAL
MEDICINES OF THE WORLD

CONTENTS

PART 2 | EASTERN ESSENTIALS

PART 3 | MAJOR PROBLEMS TCM
CAN ADDRESS

PART 4 | A GUIDE TO TCM TREATMENTS

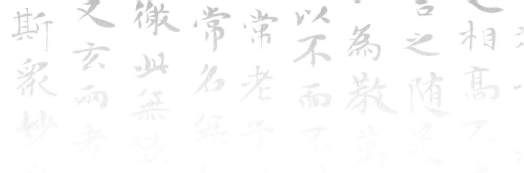

FOREWORD

Lindsey Vonn

The mountain. It's the image so many love to compare to life: Our journeys translate to "climbing the mountain." Struggles are met with pleas to go "one step at a time." Reaching a goal is making it to the "top of the mountain."

For me, mountains weren't a metaphor for life. Mountains were my life. And my mission for more than two decades: Ski down them as fast as I could.

My career as an alpine ski racer came with plenty of success, such as winning a record 82 World Cup races and three Olympic medals. But as you can imagine, there's a price to pay for high performance—especially in a sport where you're rocketing down a slope virtually unprotected. For me, that price came in the form of nine broken bones and countless surgeries on damaged body parts.

Many of my injuries, I relied on the advancement and skills of Western medicine doctors to repair my body. Without them, I wouldn't have had such a long and successful career. But as someone who has competed internationally, I have seen and respect the importance and role of traditional healing approaches, with Traditional Chinese Medicine (TCM) being especially iconic in its history and comprehensive healing techniques and artistry of anatomy.

Getting through the pain—coaxing my body back to peak performance—I explored many options to find the best solutions. My physical therapist recommended TCM therapies being tried by other world-class athletes.

Several methods played a huge role in my healing. The two I used most had explanations that were foreign to my Western Medicine-oriented mind, but I was interested in results:

>> **ACUPUNCTURE**: Using tiny needles meticulously inserted in your body to stimulate various meridians inside your body to help open the flow of Qi, the body's life force as defined by TCM.

>> **CUPPING**: Heated cups provide suction on the body to help reduce inflammation. Olympian Michael Phelps popularized this treatment in the West—you may recall seeing the large red circles on his skin (you would have seen them on me, too, but snow suits are little more modest than swimsuits!).

Here's what I've learned: It doesn't matter if you're an Olympic athlete or your main sport is tackling life. Your body responds to—and needs—different forms of therapy to help it function and recover. For me, combining Western advances and Eastern traditions is the best approach. And it's what I love about *Yin Yang You*. It's time to stop thinking of medicine as East *versus* West, but rather take an East *and* West approach to health.

And your main mission doesn't have to be zipping down a mountain at close to 100 mph to experience the benefits.

We travel though life at a variety of speeds—sometimes slaloming through obstacles, oftentimes trying to get to the top of the mountain (without the luxury of a ski lift).

To help reach your peak, it's wise to stop thinking there's only one way to heal, balance, and optimize your body.

Yin Yang You can open up your world to other ways to achieve health: Ways that will help you summit whatever mountain you're trying to conquer.

INTRODUCTION

Ancient Advances

In the few moments it takes to read these next paragraphs, you could also scroll through your Instagram feed, text "wyd" to your partner, skip a song on Spotify, click a link to see the 27 best guac recipes (ever!), and maybe even squeeze in a few seconds to record your version of the #laffytaffychallenge.

Technology has changed everything about the way we read, communicate, think, engage, and live. Yet despite all of the wonderful tools, tricks, and hacks we use every day, we also deeply crave something a little less, well, techie.

Talking to a real person not Siri or Alexa. Looking into someone's actual eyes not those googly emoji ones. Hugging a friend not thumb-tapping a photo to prove to your high school bud you like their cherry-cheesecake recipe or floppy-eared puppy.

Despite the wonders of new gadgets, we have faith in old-school wisdom. What happens if you apply the same logic to medicine?

Can we accept lessons from both new and traditional philosophies? In its century-old history, Western medicine has given us incredible advances in everything from surgical tools to diagnostic machines, antibiotics to life-saving pharmaceuticals, cutting-edge research to wow-oh-wow possibilities for extending longevity. We live longer and better because of these modern innovations.

Yet despite its exponential leaps, Western medicine does have its limitations.

Consider a recent Harris Poll that showed only 17 percent of Americans self-report to be in excellent health. An alarming number of us are plagued by low energy, high pain, and an array of problems in between. You either feel you're in excellent health, or not. There's no middle ground here. "Nah, I'm good" works if someone is offering to ladle more gravy into your gullet, not so much if you're ho-hum when asked about your health. So what's the disconnect?

In the same way technology can be blow-your-mind awesome, it doesn't resolve the basic human need for deeper human connection. Could the same be said for modern medicine? Is something missing?

When it comes to health and wellness, maybe instead of always looking to the future, we should be harvesting the past.

That past comes in the form of the 5,000-year-old art of Traditional Chinese Medicine (TCM). Common ailments (headaches, fatigue, insomnia, anxiety) have been around for millenniums, so it's perhaps a little naïve to believe remedies have only appeared in the last century.

Right now, there's no better time to explore how TCM complements the jaw-dropping advances of Western medicine. (And if your jaw aches from all that gaping, a temple and jawline massage may help.) Why?

For one, after a long history of being somewhat embarrassed by what was seen as a "backwards" approach to healing, Western-trained Chinese doctors are beginning to appreciate their heritage and have resuscitated TCM.

Secondly, it may be the right time for *you*. Sure, if you've already found a superb Western solution, then maybe your search for answers is over. But if your energy is measured in negative integers, take a look to the East.

Think about how you crave human connection—even with your phone at your fingertips. That's the way to take in TCM. We're not asking you give up your phone (Western med), but to reflect on what you may be missing if you don't seek other paths to wellness (Eastern med).

The truth is, if you're reading this book you're most likely not among that 17 percent who feel excellent. So, isn't it worth looking into methods that have worked for thousands of years?

It's true, TCM is founded on ancient discoveries, but that doesn't mean the methods are automatically outdated.

In fact, they often hold answers to medical questions—fatigue, GI troubles, depression, and many other acute conditions—you may be struggling with and have yet to find the solution. TCM also gives us exciting paths to explore major quality of life issues, such as longevity, living pain-free, and achieving holistic balance and wellness.

But let's make one thing very clear from the start. This is not a story of "either–or." This is a story of "with."

After all, that's what Yin and Yang are all about—the balance and harmony of two things working together.

Yin Yang You shows you how Eastern medicine can complement Western approaches to let you live your best, most energized, and optimal life.

✢ ✢ ✢

This book is not about pitting East and West against each other. Instead, it's created to build a bridge between Western and Eastern medicine, as depicted in the illustration on the next page. Both approaches have tremendous strengths. By keeping the best of each and discarding inefficiencies, we open the possibilities to expand services to more people, keep medical costs down, and improve health outcomes.

Yin Yang You is all about helping you integrate each approach within the realm of your personal beliefs and practices. By doing so, we hope to help societies also close the gap, so practitioners in East and West methods can work better together.

As a way to inspire your thinking about TCM, let's introduce Qi (pronounced "chee")—the life force that flows through your body and through which much of TCM revolves. Many human problems are linked to the flow of Qi. And while it's an abstract concept in TCM, some are starting to, well, quantify the role of Qi—perhaps there's a way to assess if your Qi is deficient.

Take this quiz to give you some initial insight into how TCM works and get a quick look at your Protective Qi—a specific Qi that represents the TCM concept of immunity.

DO YOU HAVE A PROTECTIVE QI DEFICIENCY?

Answer the following questions, choosing only one response for each of the five sections. Add up the points for your five answers. If your total score is 100 or over, chances are you are deficient in Protective Qi. This test is adapted with permission from the article "Development and validation of a diagnostic risk score for assessing a TCM condition, Protective Qi Deficiency, in adults." (*European Journal of Alternative Medicine*, 35:101097, 2020).

YOUR BODY, YOUR LIFE	HOW'S IT DOING?	SCORE
Your Tongue	Light red with thin white coating and is of proper size	0
	Pale in color with white coating; however, the tongue is of proper size and has no tooth marks on the sides	41
	Pale with white coating. Size is slightly larger than normal and tooth-marks are visible, but limited to part(s) of the tip and sides of the tongue	81
	Pale with white coating. Significantly larger than normal with visible tooth-marks along the full length of the tip and sides of the tongue	>100
Your Voice (when speaking to someone about six feet away)	Loud and clear	0
	Can be heard and understood, but the voice is recognizably weak	10
	Low, needs focused attention to understand	20
	Can be heard, but repeated clarification needed	30
	Cannot be heard with a clear understanding	41
How often did you catch a common cold or flu in the past two months?	No cold or flu	0
	Once	28
	Twice or more	>100
How easily do you break a sweat?	No spontaneous sweating, sweat only with intense physical activities	0
	Sweat with routine physical activities	5
	Sweat heavily with routine physical activities	10
	Sweat with slight physical activities like walking	15
	Sweat spontaneously	20

Do you have any aversion to wind and cold?	No aversion to wind or cold	0
	Aversion to wind	11
	Aversion to cold, but relieved by adding light clothing	21
	Aversion to both wind and cold (relieved by light clothing); or I'm susceptible to catch a cold when exposed to wind or cold	32
	I have aversion to cold (only relieved by thick clothing that covers whole body); or I very easily catch a cold when exposed to wind or cold	53

How'd you do? No matter where you fall, use this score as one of your diagnostic tools to assess your progress. (Yes, your blood pressure, cholesterol, waist circumference, and servings of fries you eat per week are also all excellent indicators of your overall health). Remember, we're not suggesting TCM trumps Western medicine or this Protective Qi test replaces blood immunoglobins, white blood cells, and other indicators of immunity. But it can complement Western medicine, especially for chronic issues where you lack clear answers.

You're open to this merged mindset. Now, it's time to learn more about TCM and understand its similarities and differences to Western medicine. Let's start by challenging three common assumptions many Westerners have about TCM.

WESTERN ASSUMPTION: WITHOUT CONSISTENT FORMULAS, EASTERN MEDICINE SURELY ISN'T RELIABLE.

YIN YANG YOU **ASSERTION:** EASTERN MEDICINE CREATES A FORMULA THAT WORKS FOR YOU.

One of the bigger differences between West and East centers on the relationship between physician and patient. In the East, it's less of an expert-novice interaction where the doctor prescribes the fix.

Consider TCM like the dynamic between a chef and personal diner. The chef has the expertise, with detailed knowledge of dozens of main ingredients (and their various combinations) to create countless different flavors. But instead of mass-producing 500 plates of pasta for a banquet, this chef forms a special relationship with the diner.

Think of it like this: Western medicine knows how to make pasta and can mass produce plates of pasta that will satisfy most of its customers. Serving the same dish to everyone will result in a relatively high overall success rate ("yeah, it was pretty good"). But will it be the best, tongue-tingling noodle you've ever had? Hard to say.

Eastern med knows how to make a similar dish, but does so by tinkering with spices and herbs, new ingredients, and innovative approaches—the chef intimately knows the diner's preferences. This, along with an encyclopedic knowledge of ingredients and cooking techniques, allows the chef to create a custom dish for each diner based on their specific palate.

In the same way, the Eastern physician knows each patient and their conditions intimately. Together, they combine expertise and personal experience to develop a customized approach to healing. Western medicines, by design, work for the majority, but not for everyone. (In fact, of the nearly 5,000 medications available, none purport to efficiently treat everyone with 100 percent success).

Essentially, Eastern medicine personalizes treatment, mix-and-matching the tools (herbs, acupuncture, foods, physical therapies, and more) in a unique way for every need. Based on the person, identical ailments can require vastly different healing approaches (TCM calls this "syndrome differentiation"). The TCM physician sees each patient as having a different syndrome, even if they're diagnosed with the same disease.

In TCM, the doctor makes a recipe just for *you*. It's an individual approach that puts the person or patient in the spotlight.

ASSUMPTION: SINCE TCM'S PRINCIPLES ARE ABSTRACT, IT'S A PRODUCT OF MYSTICISM AND SUPERSTITION.

YIN YANG YOU **ASSERTION:** TCM IS BASED ON A SET OF PRINCIPLES ROOTED IN ANCIENT PHILOSOPHIES ABOUT THE BODY.

When you hear TCM practices the same approach generation after generation, it's easy to brush off this information and chalk it up to being "old" and "stuck in the past." (Perhaps okay if you're talking about your cranky neighbor, but not if you're referring to TCM).

The reality is TCM originated from the idea your body, nature, and the universe all work together, as represented in the picture below. It's no coincidence the TCM "chef" utilizes tools from nature to create the right dish for you. Nature's herbs and offerings serve as the foundation for healing.

To think of your body as a universe of its own is not a novel concept. Imagine your neurons as the stars, your heart as the sun, and planets and moons existing in the form of your organs and body parts.

What a profound universe it is—with so much life, a great many abilities, and all the miraculous systems and functions enabling your existence. TCM has long held the belief that one human body is a microcosm of the universe—it functions according to the energy reflection from the sun and moon on the earth. Such energy imprints differently on various organs or systems within the human body. It works in balance—through Yin and Yang, as you will soon see. Thus, TCM doctors treat patients based on individual, seasonal, and time differences.

But here's where things expand a bit. TCM also considers the human body functions not just by itself, but also within the rhythms of nature and the universe. Just as our bodies have their own rhythms and cycles (circadian and menstrual, for example, or your post-coffee rendezvous with the commode), they also sync up with our environments.

Seasonal cycles, weather patterns, rotations around the sun. All of it.

TCM doctors see organs and their functions in the human body as reflections of the universe, meaning it's important to consider the environment in medical practice. Treatments are often recommended based on season, time of day, climate, regional environment, and so on.

At the core of TCM is a belief that individuals are an integral part of nature's power. Through careful observation of nature, the medical sages perceive patterns common to both the external environment and the internal climate of the human body have been established. Over the past 5,000 years, the cumulative considerations of practitioners has led to today's intricate TCM system of diagnosis and healing.

In contrast, Western medicine was designed to blast us off to the stratosphere of health with surgical precision. Wonderful! But we also need to tend our gardens and cultivate our crops. Ancient Chinese philosophy, with roots in Chinese agricultural civilization, emphasizes "the correspondence between man and nature," to maintain a harmonious and unified relationship for both (more on this in Chapter 2). It's why Chinese medicine is founded on five elements—wood, fire, metal, soil, and water. This intricate system reflects complex, yet orderly, "friend or foe" relationships.

For an agricultural society, connecting the fundamental energies of the environment and our body was essential to holistic survival. Many of these insights have weathered centuries of examination. They serve as an excellent prompt to consider how individual health can extend far beyond the biological boundaries of the individual body.

In a time when we are all especially sensitive to protecting the world around us, why not consider a gentler approach to caring for the world inside of us, too? This way of thinking allows us to visualize our bodies as always being in a state of flux—not simply existing as isolated body parts. This principle comes alive in treatments, techniques, and terms you will see throughout *Yin Yang You*.

ASSUMPTION: BECAUSE THE LANGUAGE IS UNFAMILIAR, THE METHODS MUST BE SUSPECT.

YIN YANG YOU **ASSERTION:** IF YOU CAN SEE THE WAY CONCEPTS TRANSLATE FROM EAST TO WEST, YOU CAN OPEN YOURSELF UP TO NEW POSSIBILITIES FOR BETTER HEALTH.

One of the big hurdles Westerners have with TCM isn't necessarily the principles. The hang-up comes when the terms used to describe certain ideas are not only diverse, they can have very different meanings than the words we know.

It's a foreign language, and yet not one you can learn on Babbel or Duolingo.

Take the kidney, for instance. In the West, we understand it as an organ that filters toxins (and as a bean that's excellent in chili). But in Chinese medicine, Kidney refers to something much bigger than a singular organ. It's a regenerating force.

Out of sheer unfamiliarity, the West sees the Chinese approach to Kidney and thinks, "Gosh, they don't even know what a simple kidney is. How the heck am I supposed to trust my body to these methods?"

To build the bridge, we must move past the translational challenges—which is why we're going to help you see Eastern concepts from a Western point of view. A Rosetta Stone®, of sorts. By untangling initial misunderstandings, you can focus on what's really important—living a healthier life.

As you work through this book, we'll help make sense of TCM through explanation and imagery and by coining new terms. You'll see how we uncode Traditional Chinese concepts to let you better embrace them and how they can work for you. (The first letters of Chinese terms are capitalized to distinguish them from our common usage). The point is, don't let these terms and names be a roadblock to knowledge. Think of this journey as not only learning about a new-for-you medical approach, but perhaps understanding a new language to help speak with your own body.

Mini Bodies on Your Body

One of the unique aspects of TCM is its system of corresponding body parts. For instance, the ear and tongue have places within these small organs that represent the whole body.

The theory is that pressing or massaging these areas can help stimulate the corresponding areas of the body. Throughout this book, you'll find references on how to stimulate small parts to help the big parts.

✛ ✛ ✛

We're bringing you on this TCM journey of discovery to introduce you to a new way of thinking. It's our hope you'll be open to new approaches for improving your health, strength, wellness, and longevity. How will we get there?

PART 1: Get the big picture about TCM. We'll sort through the difference between how the East and West approach medicine. More importantly, we'll outline how the two can work together to better your health.

You'll also be introduced to new concepts, like Qi (your life force), plus the TCM-termed Organs to carry on life forces. Learn the five elements and the different ways they interact with life force of the five different Organs. You'll see how Kidney in TCM means regenerator, how Spleen means nourisher, how Stomach means holder. (A concept not too unfamiliar for many fry-shoveling Westerners).

PART 2: Specific TCM approaches will be explained—including common treatments and foods with healing effects. You'll also learn the most fundamental principles and thinking behind Chinese medicine.

PART 3: We take a detailed look at some of the toughest topics in Western wellness—fatigue, insomnia, cold, depression, low libido, cosmetic issues, and common gastrointestinal problems—and how to approach prevention and treatment. Learn why are these conditions so difficult to solve and how a TCM mindset can help you feel better and live healthier.

PART 4: A more quick-hitting, encyclopedic approach to how TCM can help acute and chronic problems. Designed to easily flip through to find DIY TCM approaches and remedies for specific pains and conditions.

Yin Yang You brings you a unique and powerful literary and scientific collaboration. Nowhere before have such forces joined to take on the momentous task of building the bridge between Eastern and Western medicine in this way.

The team includes:

The Beijing University of Chinese Medicine—the world's most prestigious academic institution focusing on TCM. With more than 13,000 students in China and all over the world, it conducts clinical work with eight hospitals in Beijing and four other cities in China, along with four additional TCM centers in Germany, Russia, Australia, and the United States. University President Anlong Xu, Ph.D. and Associate Professor Lepeng Wang, Ph.D. harvested the institution's best wisdom for this groundbreaking book.

Mehmet Oz, M.D.—a cardiothoracic surgeon at New York Presbyterian/ Columbia University Medical Center who has long held the belief that West and East can work together for better wellness and health outcomes. For over a dozen years (and almost as many Emmy Awards), "The Dr. Oz Show" has worked to help translate complex medical topics, inspiring many paths to wellness by making tough topics accessible and actionable.

USANA Health Sciences, Inc.—internationally recognized for high-quality, science-based nutritional supplements and healthy foods, led by top industry leaders in research and innovation: Robert Sinnott, Ph.D., chief scientific officer; Jeremy Tian, Ph.D., M.D., director of new product research; Rolando Maddela, MD, MPH, executive director of nutrition research.

The *Harvard Business Review* points out health care in the United States and most other developed countries is ailing. While medical advances have been made, too many roadblocks remain surrounding costs, inefficiencies, errors, and more.

While not an abandon-everything indictment of Western medicine, doesn't it make you wonder if some solutions to age-old problems are right under our noses? Despite the best in Western medicine, some of our most common conditions often persist. Traditional therapies—those proven through trial and error for millennia—are used as a front-line approach to treat these conditions in other countries. The goal is to find a balance between the East and West approach to holistic health.

And yes, we're far from merging both worlds. Change takes time. Perhaps that's because the concepts of Qi and Yin and Yang are regarded as too esoteric and beyond the scope of experimental science. While Western medicine excels in the field of "integrative medicine," a focus on holistic healing commonly does not factor into their selection of active ingredients and compounds for drug development.

What we're truly after is not only a better understanding of TCM, but to also open the door for you to:

» Think about your health and your body in new ways.
» Explore answers to lingering questions.
» Be empowered—not just with information, but in the lessons of nature and the universe.
» Improve your internal energy to heal Organs with life force.
» Feel better, be stronger, and live longer.
» Think holistically.
» Discover your Yin and Yang.
» Find You!

PART 1

EAST & WEST

CHAPTER 1

UNMASKING
THE MYSTERY

☯

Core principles of Traditional Chinese Medicine
teach us about the whole self—and holistic health.

I n life, we seem to love a good mystery. We'll read who-done-it novels. We'll binge 27 episodes of a Netflix show filled with holy-moly cliffhangers. And we'll ask ourselves "how did they do that?" watching magicians, trick-shot artists, TikTok jokers, and bakers designing cakes mistaken for a coffee mug or tree trunk.

Mysteries, in a lot of ways, satisfy us spiritually because they pique our curiosity, arouse our senses, and fiddle with our innate human nature to keep learning.

But when it comes to our health, we like mysteries about as much as mid-scene buffering.

And for good reason. It's unsettling to *not* know what's happening with your body, whether it's a serious situation or a simple sound ("why's there a boat engine in my belly?"). In our typical medical and health universe, we end up fearing (or ignoring) mysteries. The world of the unknown, frankly, scares us.

That's perhaps one of the reasons why the West has been generally reticent about embracing TCM.

For much of the West, TCM remains a mystery. Thinking about health from a different approach feels more intimidating and unsettling than it does exciting and titillating. After all, nobody likes a cliffhanger when it comes to an itchy rash, a crippling pain, or some other bodily oddity.

It's easier—and more comforting—to stay the course with what we already know about health, about medicine, about treatments, and about diagnoses. This approach has served us well in many ways. Western medicine has given us some unimaginably innovative advances and treatments.

Yet one of our *Yin Yang You* missions is to demystify the world of TCM. Not to replace Western thinking, treatments, and approaches, but so you can learn how East and West can work together. Like Yin and Yang: in balance.

As mentioned in the book's intro, TCM has been practiced for thousands of years. It combines a number of time-tested techniques, herbal remedies, manual therapies (like acupuncture and massage), and activities (like Tai Chi) to help prevent and treat disease. This holistic approach focuses on overall wellness and longevity.

Your *Yin Yang You* journey will introduce you to concepts such as Qi and the role the universe plays in supporting your body. It begins by exploring the core principles and practices of TCM—insights, ideas, remedies, and strategies you can add to let your body speak louder for a healthier, more active, and youthful life.

Let's look at Eastern medicine's major guiding forces.

PRINCIPLE 1:
YOUR BODY WORKS IN BALANCE

Balance isn't just for gymnasts, circus performers, and branch-dancing squirrels. It has become one of the most popular catchphrases for healthy, stress-free living. "Eat a balanced diet!" "Strive for work-life balance!" "Balance your budget!" And for good reason. In general, we don't work as well when we overload our lives with too much or too little of any one thing—whether it comes to food, sleep, work, or anything really. Our bodies and minds naturally seek to live in the middle of a seesaw—not too high and not too low.

Western medicine doesn't follow this ideal as much as Eastern medicine. That's not to say it necessarily *dislikes* balance—it just doesn't dwell on it. Instead, Western medicine targets a specific problem with a specific treatment—a laser focus. For instance, with hypertension the medication is designed to bring down blood pressure, a unidirectional goal. TCM may see hypertension as Yang excess due to deficiency of Liver and Kidney Yin, and the corresponding treatment strategy is to nourish the Liver and Kidney Ying to restore the balance.

One of the primary Eastern approaches to medicine revolves around Yin and Yang: Two opposite but complementary forces working together in balance. Not too much, not too little—a true harmonious state. This notion is common in modern science—positive and negative charges or forces and counterforces in physics, for example. And we've all heard the term "opposites attract."

In Chinese culture, Yin and Yang symbolize many kinds of opposite forces—male and female, positive and negative, strong and weak, spiritual and material, joy and worry, sunrise and sunset. The same holds true from a medical perspective. In TCM, everything is classified under one of two divisions—exterior and interior, the abdomen and the back, diseases from external causes and diseases from internal causes. Remedies are based on restoring balance.

The body should work like a smooth dance between Yin and Yang. The dancers move in unison, though technically, they're moving in opposite ways. While one is stepping to the left, the other steps to the right, or one to the front, the other to the back.

When done well, it's beautiful to behold—smooth, together, complementary. And when out of sync, it appears clunky, off, chaotic. The same holds true for the body. It operates much better when the opposing forces are waltzing *together* in rhythm.

How does Yin and Yang look in Eastern medicine? Treatments and approaches always consider the whole body and both forces, not just one isolated issue. Healing techniques continually strive for a sense of biological equilibrium, driven by internal life force throughout the body.

Yin-Yang is such a fundamental idea in TCM that *anything* is divided into Yin and Yang. This overarching concept leads to a holistic view of the body distinct from that of Western medicine. TCM doesn't see the body as a collection of individual cells, organs, tissues, and systems, but an integrated entity that has a unified Yin and Yang dynamics.

This makes sense when you consider all organs in the human body are connected—meaning disease spreads throughout the body, as does good health. If a part of the body has an issue, TCM sees it as a whole body Yin-Yang imbalance. It's why TCM doctors treat the whole body, not just one organ or medical problem.

For this reason, TCM characteristically characteristically refers to a disease as a "syndrome," a term quite different from that used in Western medicine. In TCM's view, anything that goes awry is reflected in a multifaceted way by the whole body.

Fittingly, TCM treats patients with a unique holistic principle. A few minutes of kneading at the acupoint on the wrist (called Neiguan, about four fingers' width above the horizontal line of your wrists and between the two outer tendons, see page 134) helps to relieve headache and some seemingly unrelated symptoms, such as low libido, diarrhea, and hemorrhoids (sure to bring on a headache for any Western doctor who tries to make sense of it).

PRINCIPLE 2:
YOUR BODY HAS A LIFE FORCE

Pop quiz: What's the central unit of your body? Some may say the brain. Adolescent boys may choose another organ. Still others might blurt out, "The heart!" If you were in a Western anatomy class, you'd get a gold star. After all, it's the heart that beats, pumps blood, and in many ways, serves as our primary life-sustaining organ.

Not to downplay or diminish the outstanding achievements of our favorite muscular thumper, but TCM doesn't think about the body in the same way. Instead, the correct answer would be Qi.

In TCM, Qi is the most basic building block of human activity (illus-

trated here as a form of energy) as well as substance. Some call it the "vital energy." We will explore Qi in depth in Chapter 4, but it is worth noting here because it's central to TCM thinking. That is, we all inherit some of our Qi through our parents, but we also have the ability to build and strengthen it as a way to improve our long-term health and wellness.

Now, you may be thinking, "Pff, Qi may be a good Scrabble word, but what does it really do for my body?" Here's the thing: Qi isn't some form of voodoo or magic. But it is a more intangible concept than the way we tend to think about how our bodies work. Qi transfers life force in ways analogous to Western medicine's understanding of gene expression, molecule synthesis, molecular functions, blood and fluid circulation, and organ function.

Later in this book, you'll get a crash course in TCM to expand on ideas you may have heard of but may not know much about. This includes Qi, but also introduces the five elements (what the heck does fire have to do with your heart?). And we'll explore the concept of meridians—the webs through which life energy flows. Instead of focusing on a specific ailment or condition in your body, there's a bigger picture—one that goes a long way in determining your overall health.

It's your Qi. Think of it as your biological swagger.

A Piercing Problem

One of the major techniques of TCM is acupoints. Held together by meridians—highways that connect one body part to another and pathways for your Qi—acupoints can be massaged, pressed, and otherwise manipulated to help ease pain in various parts of the body. For example, pressing a certain part of your foot (mostly acupoints) can relieve headaches via these meridians. So it's interesting to note that some in TCM believe piercing the ears—especially in non-lob parts of the ear—can have a negative effect on your health. That's because the ear is part of the complex meridian system, and piercings are believed to cause a disruption in the flow of Qi and other body fluids. While we're not advocating a pierce-free zone, it's interesting to see how the body is connected in ways we may not normally think about.

PRINCIPLE 3: PREVENTION SITS ATOP THE HIERARCHY

Here's a stunning fact: There are doctors in TCM dedicated to keeping you well. In fact, they may even treat you for free if you get sick—underscoring the point that wellness is the primary focus. TCM hospitals in China have specialized departments called "treating the yet-to-be sick." This comes from a famous quote from the oldest TCM scripture: "The best doctors treat patients who are yet-to-be sick."

This insight lies at the heart of how TCM approaches wellness. The key to living long and strong is to treat your body before it gets sick—by thinking about Yin and Yang, improving protective Qi, and perceiving how the body is affected by the world's cycles and rhythms (well-connected to seasonal and nocturnal changes).

While Western medicine has certainly placed an emphasis on prevention with a focus on healthy diet and exercise, the statistics show the message isn't resonating. In the U.S., 69 percent of Americans are overweight or obese, and 43 percent have or are at risk for type 2 diabetes, with the majority completely unaware. And 45 percent have some form of cardiovascular disease. It's one of the reasons why Covid-19 hit so aggressively. All of these numbers can be lowered if people comply with prevention recommendations.

For cultures that practice TCM, the statistics look quite a bit different: The obesity rate in China is about 16 percent—less than half the 35 percent in the U.S. That doesn't mean TCM is the only reason. We look at a variety of variables such as genetics, environment, and other factors (U.S. fast-food chains seem to pop up faster than teenage pimples). Maybe it's simply that China is slowly catching up to the U.S. The point is, obesity stats are complex, but it does make you wonder if TCM is a contributing factor to overall wellness.

Prevention of chronic ailments is the best way to treat them—that is, never having to *really* treat them in the first place.

The primary responsibility of the TCM physician is to keep people well or intervene at early stages when imbalance/dysfunction is suspected or detected. This is possible because the disruption of Yin and Yang often comes before the emergence of symptoms, allowing TCM to address problems not yet apparent to the patient. The idea is for doctors to treat diseases before they start to develop—nipping them at the "bud stage"— which not only helps the individual, but also lessens pressure on the societal medical system.

Mini Bodies on Your Body

As you will learn, TCM is guided by various Yin and Yang elements—for instance, Heat and Coolness—and how these elements play a role in your health. Because so much of TCM practice allows for self-care, it's interesting to see various recommended practices, such as these:

Wash your face in cold water. Do it twice a day to help increase blood circulation of the face and increase cold tolerance to help prevent future colds.

Use your hair dryer— on your neck. Position your hair dryer at the base of your neck and allow warm air to blow up to your neck area. This promotes warmth and helps relieve cold symptoms.

PRINCIPLE 4: YOU HAVE POWER

For many reasons, the West's structure of medicine is pretty clear when it comes to regulation of medications, treatments of diseases, and the curious case of why physician handwriting is so illegible.

However, this clear structure is based on the knowledge of physics, chemistry, and biology, not the philosophy of Yin and Yang and Qi. The doctor is the expert with the knowledge, credentials, and skills. Their process is mechanically, chemically, and/or biologically clear—symptom, diagnosis, treatment—but does not necessarily lead to an intrinsic understanding of the lives of their patients. What does the patient bring to the table? In Western medicine, the patient/doctor relationship is more of an expert versus customer one than a partnership. You tell doctors your symptoms ("it's very itchy!"), they make an educated guess ("it looks like eczema") and write you a script ("here's a corticosteroid"), and that's it until next time ("thanks, doc!"). Think of it as the most expensive "drive-thru transaction" you'll ever make.

We're not saying it's a wrong approach. It's simply the way the system works, and very successfully in many cases—especially when it comes to treating serious issues like heart surgery, brain trauma, orthopedic injuries, and more.

The TCM approach skews a little more to a balanced (yes, there's the Yin and Yang again) perspective in treatment. It creates a partnership between doctor and patient, looking at the root of medical problems through conversation and TCM diagnosis. And this approach works incredibly well for chronic issues, like prediabetic syndrome, asthma, allergies, fatigue, bowel problems, chronic pain, and others. It requires a close doctor-patient relationship—the patient's personality, temper, mood, even favorite color and food, etc. all contribute to the doctor's evaluation and treatment.

In TCM, the physician and patient work together to consider, evaluate, treat, and prevent all issues of health and wellness. That doesn't mean the West doesn't do this (in fact, we're seeing more and more wellness-coach relationships forming). Quite simply, it's a foundational principle of TCM to place more emphasis on the idea that you are a partner in your own health and medical treatments, not a passive recipient of care and prescriptions.

There's a suggestion the patient would also have to take up responsibility to work with the doctor to achieve optimal results. But it may be out of context.

This leads us back to the "You" in *Yin Yang You*. You have the power to:

» Balance your body.

» Harmonize your approach between East and West.

» Strengthen your Qi.

» Fine-tune your Yin and Yang.

» Improve the way your body operates in this great big world of ours—and yours.

» Find You!

Does Everyone in China use TCM?

In the long history of China, everyone used TCM. However, this hasn't been the case since 1840.

Although TCM is an old concept, it's actually regaining traction in China. A short historical reason: The Opium War in 1840 and Sino-Japanese War in 1894-5 led to the end of the Qin Dynasty and the beginning of the Republic of China in 1911. For the next century, Western medicine gradually overtook TCM as Chinese people began to lose confidence in their cultural heritage. The dogma established TCM as a reflection of backward ways that needed to be upgraded by modern science and technology.

Most preferentially choose Western medicine over TCM (up to 80 percent opt for Western medicine first when they have an ailment to treat). This is because they don't have well-suited Chinese traditional culture education and are overwhelmed by Westernized thoughts about health and diseases.

Fortunately, the new generation of leaders appreciate the value of preserving a 5,000-year-old tradition of healing and have reversed the approach. TCM is blossoming again as a fundamental platform for reviving traditional healing practices both in China and around the world.

Anytime we're challenging our own long-held beliefs, it can feel like trying to squeeze into our high-school jeans: a little bit uncomfortable. We have open ourselves to the idea that what we thought was one way actually isn't that way at all. As you explore your future relationship with TCM, start by breaking down barriers about what you assume to be true.

CHAPTER 2

EAST VS. WEST

☯

Understanding the differences between the
two schools of medical thought lays the foundation
for how they can work together

You don't need us to paint a detailed picture of one of the most common symptoms people feel today: fatigue. After all, when you start to
type "why am I" into the Google search bar, the first thing that auto-pop-
ulates to predict your thought is "so tired."

The truth is, you already know what fatigue—in its many forms—feels
like. Some days you can't keep your eyes open past 7 p.m. There are morn-
ings you hit your snooze button with such felonious contempt you could
get cuffed for third-degree assault. At times, your body feels like it's been
churned through a washing machine's spin cycle 519 times. Sometimes, it
takes Herculean strength to brush your teeth. And some days your energy
feels like a 20-watt bulb with the responsibility of lighting up an entire city.

Feeling this way over and over and over, day after day after day takes its toll. You wonder, and you worry. And you may decide to seek some help from someone other than the almighty Google to get answers why you feel like one, tiny smooshed grape in the produce aisle of life.

For the sake of learning the difference in approaches between Western and Eastern medicine, let's take this symptom to an office that has two doors: one side East, one side West.

How would each method go about finding what's wrong?

In the Western office, your health professional would approach this like a medical mystery. After all, there are literally dozens and dozens of conditions where fatigue is a symptom. It could be hormonal (hypothyroidism). It could be psychological (depression). It could be chemical (anemia). It could be infectious (we're all too familiar with Covid-19). And it could be innumerable other physical and mental pathologies, ranging from cancer and heart disease to insomnia and sleep apnea.

And so, the Western health pro would start with an investigation—first asking you about family history, your medical history, other symptoms you may have, and any other clues as to what is causing the fatigue. Based on this info, they may have their suspicions as to what's going on, but they'll want some hard data to confirm.

You'll likely have a series of diagnostics—most certainly a blood test that can identify deficiencies of some sort (hormones, vitamins, nutrients). If there's a clear picture of what could be the root cause, you could be prescribed a medication, a dietary change, vitamins, or other medical solution (C-PAP machine for sleep apnea, iron infusion for anemia). You may also be instructed on lifestyle choices that can help (better diet, improving sleep hygiene, watching caffeine consumption, stress-management techniques).

There's a good chance the picture may not be immediately clear, because fatigue is such a ubiquitous manifestation of so many problems. It's also worth noting, this is a simplified version of a complex issue and this process—from symptom to diagnosis—will likely not happen in one visit, or even at all, in which case doctors put you under a convenient category, "Chronic Fatigue Syndrome." But in short, the door with the West sign hanging from it takes a "checklist" approach—ruling out some causes and focusing in on others, whatever the clues dictate. Find the problem, fix the problem.

In the Eastern medicine office, fatigue is attributed to various root problems in its unique Organ system understanding. It could be Spleen Qi deficiency, Kidney Yang deficiency, and Heart Blood deficiency, just to name a few. A defining difference with TCM is all problems are seen to result from a loss of balance. Deficiency is the loss of weight on one side of balance, regardless of the location (Spleen, Kidney, or Heart) or the nature (Qi, Yang, or Blood). And since Yin and Yang is the essence of balance, it brings us back to the fundamentals of TCM.

To assess balance, your doctor will look at your whole body—your posture, the way you walk into the room, the color of your tongue and lips, the strength of your pulse, etc. And no matter the specific cause at the organ or chemical level a Western doc may find, the TCM treatment will restore balance by strengthening the Spleen Qi, elevating Kidney Yang, and nourishing the Blood…all this to eventually reverse fatigue in the process.

The big difference is, while there may be an identifiable reason for feeling fatigued, the body works holistically—treating the entire being will also treat the micro-problem. The elegance of the TCM solution lies in its simplicity. Balancing Yin and Yang holistically treats the body while addressing the fatigue.

We will explore causes and treatments of fatigue in depth later in the book. Our main mission here is to shine a spotlight on the differences between how the two approaches work. One is not better than the other necessarily, they're simply different.

You've gotten a taste of differences between East and West in Chapter 1 and in the above scenario, but it's worth unpacking a bit more here. Why? Our goal is to not have competing interests, but complementary ones. As you understand how they contrast, you'll begin to see the possibility of a hybrid medical system where the two medical approaches could coexist (this is the subject of Chapter 3).

THE FOUR MAIN PHILOSOPHICAL DIFFERENCES:

THE WESTERN MEDICAL SYSTEM IS CENTRAL TO A HUNTING-AND-FISHING PHILOSOPHY.

THE EASTERN MEDICAL SYSTEM CENTERS AROUND A FARMING PHILOSOPHY.

Think about these two schools of thought. In hunting and fishing, there's a winner and loser—the predator and the prey. The rules are governed by the laws of the jungle and survival of the fittest. To survive, you need to fight, control, and conquer nature.

The same goes for the general Western approach to medicine—everything in the universe can be divided into smaller parts, with competing interests among those parts. You beat toxic cells or they beat you. You stalk disease or disease defeats you.

To win these micro wars, Western philosophy uses logic, science, and rationality. We see this in the treatment of a specific disease, therapies used with pinpoint precision, targeted analysis, and scientific methods. In fact, Western medicine has developed into a complete medical system based on human anatomy and the physical, chemical, and biological dissection of life into microparts. Locate the problem, define the source and symptoms, and eliminate the problem with aimed theories. Law of the jungle.

Locate the prey, kill the prey, live to fight another day.

Eastern medicine employs more of a farming philosophy (not surprising, as it's the root of Chinese civilization). In farming, there's no predator vs. prey dynamic—it's about working in harmony with the land.

Ancient Chinese philosophy emphasizes "the correspondence between man and nature"—that is, to maintain a unified relationship between the two.

This belief values contemplation, perception, inspiration, and insight. The Eastern mode of thinking is a macro perception on human life, rather than a micro view. It encompasses everything about Chinese medicine and the unity between man and nature to examine the holistic relationships in the world we live. TCM treats diseases by focusing on "the diseased person," seeing the human body as small universe, rather than evaluating the "diseased organ/tissue of person." It is no wonder, with this way of thinking, why surgery doesn't prosper as a major therapy.

The farmer works with the land, not against it.

Plant the seeds, work with the land, nurture the crop.

WESTERN ORGANS ARE PHYSICAL.

EASTERN ORGANS ARE FUNCTIONAL.

Flashback to biology class (dissected frogs and all), and you'll quickly remember how the West views organs. They're physical entities—each with its own job. Right? Even if you've never peered into an open bodily cavity, you have an idea of how every organ looks and what they do.

The heart thumps and pumps and delivers blood throughout your body. Your colon looks like a large worm and is responsible for discharge of undigested food. You can see your kidneys, your liver, your brain, your *everything*. Western medicine has broken down the body by its parts, and those parts are treated when they can't do their job.

This is one of the biggest roadblocks when it comes to the West understanding the East. In Eastern medicine, Organs aren't seen as physical structures, their role is much bigger—with a greater emphasis on whole-body function, rather than a one-organ-one-job approach. Think about it this way: In Western medicine organs have functions that overlap, while in TCM they function as one abstract Organ.

Take Heart as an example. Belonging to the element of fire, the Heart is one of five life energy movements defined by TCM (we'll explain more in Chapter 4). In Western medicine, the main physiological function of the heart is a pump that drives blood flow. It pushes blood to the artery and pulls the blood in from the vein. As a major part of the circulatory system, it's an anatomically defined organ that's separate from other parts of the system: artery, vein, capillary vessels, and the blood.

In contrast, the TCM Heart is a synonym of almost the entire circulatory system. It embraces everything involved in bringing blood rich in nutrients to the tissues and carrying the blood with waste away. Visualize the circulatory system as a heading with all its subheads: heart, blood vessels, and the blood.

Notice, however, the circulatory system in Western medicine is not limited to blood circulation. For instance, it has chemo-sensing activity in the carotid body that detects any change of oxygen level in the blood, hence regulating breathing. And the blood has a large number of immune cells that are part of the immune system. These non-circulatory activities are not considered as part of the TCM Heart.

Let's look at Spleen as another example. In Western med, spleen is a concrete organ located in the upper-left abdominal cavity. It serves as a reservoir to store large numbers of immune cells and also specializes in clearing worn-out blood cells.

The TCM Spleen is completely different. It's an Organ that "transforms and transports." And it welcomes everything involved in digestion and absorption—including nearly the entire digestive tract, from the mouth to anus, and digestive glands such as the liver and pancreas. It could even cover some of the microbiome functions.

In Western medicine, however, the digestive tract is not limited to digestion and absorption. It's also closely related to some activities of the immune and nervous system. But in TCM Spleen *only* includes its part of digestion and absorption.

As we discuss TCM Organs throughout the book, it will be from the context of their whole-body functions of inter-playing Organs, not as the physical, separated structures from biology class.

WESTERN MEDICINE = REDUCTIONISM

EASTERN MEDICINE = HOLISM

If you're wondering what reductionism is, it has nothing to do with a balsamic glaze. In this context, it's about a philosophy. Specifically, it's the intellectual and philosophical position that a complex system is the sum of its parts. This is a core value of the scientific method—reducing a big picture to simple objects for processing. And this is how Western medicine works: Explain a complex system by the sum of its parts and interactions.

Ask a question → Put forth a hypothesis → Conduct an experiment → Collect data → Draw a conclusion

As we put this process in motion, it becomes clear the Western medical approach uses this same method over and over and over again—with animal subjects, small numbers of human subjects, bigger numbers of human subjects, and so on. Taking a deeper look, every facet of a medical issue is deconstructed this way: It's not just one study about heart disease. It's a zillion studies about every facet of heart disease—whether it's about medication or diet or surgical procedures or anything. Breaking down the big picture into small-scale pieces allows conclusions to be drawn by analyzing the smaller parts. A puzzle comes together with a thousand pieces. That's reductionism.

Going back to the fatigue example: Test the thyroid, treat the thyroid. That doesn't work, try vitamin B12 injections. Maybe add in sleep hygiene changes and a regular exercise routine.

It totally makes sense. But there's a drawback. Often, the individual pieces interact with each other. So after you break one piece from others, it's not exactly the same as it was when they were connected. It's like a caveman looking at a light bulb and a power switch. Only when he screws in the bulb does he realize the light can be turned on.

On the other hand, Chinese medicine employs a holism philosophy. Holism is the idea that various systems (e.g. physical, biological, social) should be viewed as wholes, not merely as a collection of parts. Holism advocates that each part of a system (such as the universe, human body, etc.) is an organic whole and cannot be divided or understood separately. Systems are approached as coherent entity.

For example, when investigating a complex machine, a reductionist may immediately take up a screwdriver to disassemble the machine into thousands of parts and inspect them separately. This is obviously time-consuming, and not necessarily ideal. Holism takes a simpler approach. They look to understand the overall functions of the system, but are not overly concerned about how the small parts affect how the system works. This is the rationale behind TCM's unique way of conceptualizing Organs by function, instead of anatomy.

A holistic approach allows practitioners to embrace the human body as a complex living individual composed of multiple systems. With each system cooperating closely to maintain the orderly and normal operation of life activities. (Recent studies show microbial communities—bacteria, fungus, viruses, etc.—parasitized in the body or on its surface are closely involved in the development of various systems and are considered to be part of the body's ecosystem, substantiating TCM's holistic view).

WESTERN MEDICINE USES MASS TREATMENTS FOR INDIVIDUALS.

EASTERN MEDICINE USES INDIVIDUAL TREATMENTS FOR THE MASSES.

In the West, the path to a cure works like this: problem exists, the scientific community researches the problem and hypothesizes various treatments. After a long road of testing, experimentation, implementation, and development, approved treatments become part of standard protocol. This strategy is used for drugs, surgery, and even lifestyle changes. The goal is to discover treatments with a high rate of efficacy (no medication or surgery is 100 percent effective), low rate of risk or damage, and minimal side effects. When this standard is reached, it becomes the "mass" treatment for disease—the primary way doctors treat a certain disease or condition for the majority of their patients. A major side benefit of standardizing diagnosis and treatment is that medical schools can also standardize training. If you know the "right" answer, you graduate. The one side effect is this may inadvertently produce cookie-cutter clinicians who can have trouble looking at problems from diverse perspectives.

TCM does it differently. By looking at the whole picture of the person, TCM doctors give individual diagnoses and treatments. There are literally dozens and dozens of different TCM prescriptions for the same symptoms defined by Western medicine. That's because the "N of 1" (the individual) dictates the treatment. When Western researchers share data, they take pride in the number of people, or N value in the study. The scientist with an N of 1,000 gets bragging rights over the scientist with an N of 23 (and they know how to rub it in).

On the flip side, the N of 1 honored in Eastern medicine is one of much lower study significance in the West, because it simply represents a case study or anecdotal evidence—not necessarily something worthy of sharing with the masses. Training experts in this approach is also more challenging, as success is sometimes in the eye of the beholder. Thus, a TCM practitioner's excellence is ultimately appraised by their patients, not by a so-called standard test. How do you know if an artist is well-enough trained?

In Chapter 5, you'll see how a TCM doctor differentiates patients with a common symptom in their unique process of diagnosis, and how they prescribe a treatment based on numerous individualized factors.

EAST VS. WEST CHEAT SHEET

East	West
Emphasizes balance of the body (i.e. rebuild a defense system to survive with a tumor). This is rooted between the two sides of Yin and Yang (neither too much or too little) existing in a harmonious state (homeostasis).	Body is a battlefield where medicine fights disease (i.e. destroys the cancer so the body can recover).
Treats problems broadly to combat "disease features" (patterns of symptoms and signs that reflect the nature of disease), rather than minute molecules.	Develops new drugs that target specific molecules with clear mechanisms for effectiveness.
The sage treats the disease before the disease develops.	The expert treats the disease after symptoms appear.
Physiology / pathology / treatment are affected by season, climate, regional environment, and so on.	Most diseases have specific treatment protocols regardless of climate or environment.
Uses imagery and natural elements of life energy movement to describe pathologies and treatments, as seen in the five elements (see Chapter 4) and images of sun rising and setting.	The use of analogy and imagery is a relatively new way for Western medicine to help patients understand disease and the body. The two "dictionaries" of imagery differ between the cultures, making it harder for the West to understand Eastern terminology.

> ## Wonders of the World
>
> Some plants are known to have changed their colors to give themselves camouflage protection from herbivores. Now, *Smithsonian Magazine* reports botanists have identified one species that seems to have performed the same trick to hide from humans. *Fritillaria delavayi* grows on the rocky slopes of China's Hengduan Mountains and its bright green foliage with yellow flowers usually stands out from the surrounding gray hillside. The plant has long been harvested for use in TCM, but in recent years, as demand for the herb has increased, it has become increasingly hard for pickers to find. Botanists found that *Fritillaria delavayi* hadn't disappeared, but had instead developed a camouflage: gray and brown leaves to match the rocky surface beneath them. By interviewing pickers to determine the areas where the plant was most heavily harvested and measuring how closely the leaves matched those environments, researchers concluded that human activity had driven this evolutionary shift.

IS TCM STUCK IN THE PAST?

While the placebo effect—the belief that a treatment works rather than having clinical proof to show it does—is real. It doesn't mean this is true for TCM treatments. Some researchers have tried to prove Eastern treatments work only by placebo effect.

Many randomized, controlled studies in world-leading medical journals have shown the effect of TCM is far superior to placebo. For example, a systematic review of 23 randomized studies that looked at the effectiveness of TCM on chronic fatigue syndrome found TCM is effective for alleviating symptoms.

Passed along for many generations, TCM offers practical experience for preventing and curing diseases. There are a few key caveats:

1) TCM HISTORICALLY DOESN'T DO TRIALS. Only recently has the concept of clinical trials begun to gain momentum. While there are now thousands of trials involving TCM, it's only a tiny number compared with Western medicine. An even smaller number of studies are conducted for prevention, which is where the strength of TCM lies.

2) TCM THERAPY IS HIGHLY PERSONALIZED. For the same condition, treatment may vary by person. This individualized approach makes conducting trials difficult.

3) TCM THERAPIES ARE IDEALLY TESTED ON TCM TERMS. Given TCM sees health and disease from fundamentally distinct perspectives, a TCM therapy should be studied with outcomes based on a TCM principle.

TCM is not some form of dark art. Instead, it represents the accumulated knowledge of millions of agrarian people over thousands of years of living under tough circumstances with only the resources at hand to help them survive. While not everything has been the subject of double-blind, placebo-controlled clinical studies, it doesn't mean it's quackery. The truth is there are very few Western medicines that have stood the test of hundreds—even thousands—of years and been used by millions of satisfied customers.

Even some Western medicines that have been through a full, rigorous FDA approval process have been recalled due to unanticipated side effects. The big issue for TCM in the West is ensuring quality control from manufacturers to users. But the fact of the matter is, like Western medicine, TCM is built upon creating patterns of diagnosis and care—they just use different language and philosophical thinking.

As mentioned above, researchers are taking more rigorous approaches to investigate TCM therapies. Just like pharmaceutical trials, this gets expensive, so creating private and public sector partnerships really helps underwrite this profoundly important research. For instance, in a recent study University researchers worked with Dr. Tian's company in the private sector to create a gold standard (placebo-controlled, randomized, and double-blinded) protocol. It was developed to test the effect of a natural compound β-glucan on Protective Qi deficiency (a TCM condition where patients tend to have a cold or flu). β-glucan is rich in food sources like mushroom, oat, and yeast and has been reported to enhance immunity. The participants were all patients of Protective Qi deficiency and took either β-glucan or placebo pills twice a day for three months. What happened? β-glucan improved Protective Qi within one month of treatment, and this effect lasted throughout the study. Studies like this have far-reaching significance. They go a long way toward answering two relevant questions:

1. **DOES TCM DO RESEARCH?** While it's true that since its inception TCM therapies have relied predominantly upon observational evidence, novel interventional studies like this one are taking off to help further advance TCM therapeutics.

2. **ARE TCM DRUGS ALL OLD SCHOOL?** In other words . . . since TCM pharmacopeia was established a long time ago and are mostly based on herbs, does TCM develop new drugs like big pharmas do? This study helps to answer this question by testing a chemically defined compound as a novel TCM therapy. It'll be an exciting prospect in the future for TCM to see Western medicine as a repertoire of new drugs and tap into it for drug development, just as the West does to advance its drug formulations.

Eastern medicine can be positioned as the frontline approach to keep people well and help manage chronic and preventable conditions, while Western medicine approaches can be used efficiently to intervene should these approaches fail. Over time, we are hopeful these approaches overlap more. As the West begins to understand the importance of prevention, TCM therapies will be used for wide-scale, cost-effective treatment of serious ailments like artemisinin for malaria—the discovery that won the 2015 Nobel Prize in Physiology or Medicine.

CHAPTER 3

EAST WITH WEST

*Why the future of medicine should use both methods
for overall health, wellness, and longevity*

Remember the two doors we looked at in the last chapter? One for Eastern medicine and one for Western?

Now we want you to think of one connected door—a door that opens up to a world that maximizes the strength of both medical approaches. One that allows you to take advantage of the best of both worlds to:

» Fix problems you have
» Prevent problems you're yet to have
» Optimize and balance your body
» Operate at high energy
» Feel well-nourished, strong, and young
» Peacefully exist in your own biological universe
» Feel *good*!

That's the unified door we envision. We believe you can achieve this goal with Eastern and Western working together in a hybrid system. To visualize how this might happen, it makes sense to take a look at, well, an actual door.

Let's say this door has a couple of issues. The doorknob squeaks and the door sticks a little, making it tough to open. Western medicine would tighten the screws of the knob to fix the problem. Eastern medicine would use a grease or material that seems to have worked for millennia to stop the squeaking (they'd fix the issue, but perhaps use a different tool).

The stickiness of the door is another good example of how they'd both approach the same problem differently.

> » The Western carpenter sees the telltale sign (friction mark) on the door and says: "Aha, the door doesn't fit the frame."
> » In contrast, the TCM doctor looks at the ground and notices some buckling or cracking there. He determines the problem comes from the settling ground causing the frame to warp.

Both diagnoses are correct. While the Western approach is more direct and has a higher degree of certainty, TCM gets to the root of the problem.

Next, the two carpenters would understandably take different measures based on their diagnoses.

> » The West carpenter would adjust the hinge, chisel off the rubbing spot on the door, or even replace the door. All that work to eliminate the friction.
> » The TCM carpenter would try to level the ground so the door will not stick now, and even in the future.

This shows the spirit of TCM that seeks to "treat the cause of the problem as well as the symptoms." It's exciting to note: both measures could be taken on the same door without hampering the other. That's a "hybrid system."

Going further, Eastern medicine would also take a step back to ask if you even need a door in the first place. It might even suggest you use a curtain in this space rather than a solid door. And it would take it a step forward to ask if the color of the door is really what gives you the most pleasure. It would say you could change the handle based on both aesthetics and function. It might even say you could put a small window in the door to help maximize light and enhance your enjoyment by seeing what's on the other side. It would center its thinking on the door—not only on the problem, but everything about it.

See how the Eastern approach addresses the door from both a system design and style design? Big-picture value and feel-good value. It's a more layered and nuanced approach that goes beyond a make-the-knob-work-better solution to a place that makes the door the best door possible.

This is ultimately what this connection can achieve: The medical advances of the West combined with the stylized and systematic strategies of the East can make you and your body the best it can be.

✝ ✝ ✝

The real secret to integrating Eastern medicine is challenging our assumptions about tools and fixes. TCM tools don't just exist to fix what's broken. They exist to prevent stuff from being broken in the first place. They also hold us back from myopically loving our hammer so much that we look for nails to strike to fix every problem. After all, not every illness is caused by a loose nail. And we waste resources searching for a nail when the real problem is rotten wood, or has nothing to do with carpentry at all.

When you expand the possibilities for how you live and approach prevention and treatment, you give yourself a much better chance for a life of optimum health.

It's not East vs. West. It's East *with* West.

We're calling for a hybrid system where people can flow between Eastern and Western medical approaches, depending on the issues, questions, or goals you have. Every person, attitude, tolerance level, body, and health issue is a bit different. And creating a hybrid system is not easy.

It should be said that hybrid systems already do exist. They're in use throughout the United States, Canada, Europe, and other Western countries, but they're not widespread. For example, the Scripps Center for

Integrative Medicine in San Diego, California and several other notable programs apply both Western and Eastern medical approaches. And the prestigious Beijing University of Chinese Medicine, who is co-authoring this book, already has a branch in the state of Maryland and has successfully provided high-quality TCM in South Munich, Germany for 30 years.

For issues such as chronic pain management, some percentage of patients will respond to gentle treatments such as acupuncture, moxibustion (which you'll read about on page 77), or herbal treatments, which are safer and have fewer side effects than commonly used NSAIDs and opioids. Or another way to think about it: While Western medicine offers intermittent fasting as a way to address obesity, TCM might prescribe a specific category of food to rebalance Qi—a result that prevents obesity-related heart diseases, but is not swiftly measured on a scale.

The beauty of the hybrid system is, by accepting TCM as valid (not just a placebo effect as many Western-trained physicians believe) it opens up a whole arsenal of safe, inexpensive treatments we can use to clear some of the non-life-threatening cases overburdening our health care systems. And a lot of supportive data generated over the past 5,000 years, and especially over the past few decades, has been hidden from the West.

In a 1971 *New York Times* article, writer James Reston heralded his appendectomy that took place as Nixon was opening China. He skillfully explains how Chinese doctors used acupuncture and herbs to conduct his operation. All of a sudden, Americans realized this was not some backward remnant of history, but rather a medical system that had been lost or hidden from us for years.

Can TCM solve everything? Of course not.

Could it help with some of our health care expenses? Certainly so.

And if it did, it could mean an annual savings of almost $1 trillion per year in the U.S. alone, based on 2019 figures.

Here are some ways of thinking about a hybrid medical approach—possibilities that would allow the strengths of Eastern and Western medicine to coexist in your life.

THINK IN SHADES OF GRAY

We know books with "shades" and "gray" in their title are very different from this one. Nevertheless, the deeper message underlines a titillating academic observation. Part of our challenge is trying to communicate the benefits of Eastern medicine in the confines of our societal-driven, concrete, black-or-white terms—you have a disease or you don't; you're healthy or you're not; the treatment works or it doesn't; you have high blood pressure or you don't.

This way of thinking is all well and good in many, many scenarios. You're either positive or negative for Covid-19. Your heart valve is well-functioning or it's not. Your appendix is healthy or it's about to burst like a Yellowstone geyser. Western medicine treats—and fixes—many issues like this. And it's a major reason why we can live longer and stay healthier.

However, many of us are mired in a mud pit of chronic problems—problems that seem to have few answers and greatly affect our quality of life and overall health. This is where Eastern medicine's strength lies: In the many shades of gray.

Mood, fatigue, and pain, for example.

Sure, Western medicine does have its options. But Eastern medicine tends to be better equipped to address the subtleties of some of these lingering and often hard to measure ailments.

How's it possible then that a millennium-old medicine has more subtlety than modern medicine? As you know, everything in TCM hangs on the balance of Yin and Yang. It's a subtle moment when the balance starts to sway. Things are seemingly fine. No symptoms. It is a stage that disease-oriented Western medicine doesn't have a good grip on. However, this is where TCM has focused since its inception.

TCM attributes chronic illnesses to an initial beginning of deficiency, namely, one side of the balance has lost weight. A deficiency could happen in various forms (such as deficiency of Yin, Yang, Qi, or Blood) and at any Organs (such as Spleen or Kidney deficiency). TCM sees this as the trickle that becomes a raging river if not tended to. And accordingly, TCM has developed a rich repertoire of strategies to deal with it. The point here is, there's a gap between the initial imbalance and the disease. It's a shade of gray where TCM has an advantage over Western medicine.

We aren't machines or cars or robots, which means every problem isn't one troubleshooting guide away from being solved. As a living ecosystem with our own universe of cells, organs, and systems, our complex bodies react much more subtly to disease, to change, to stress, to life.

Let the power of the Western scientific community extend your life and tackle some of life's toughest challenges: heart attacks, tumors, traumatic injuries, and the like. But also let the power of the Eastern methods help you see that your body is different from everyone else's. And just maybe in those shades of gray you'll find the solutions you've been searching for—along with extending your life—to tackle some of life's other challenges.

EMBRACE THE PRECISION OF PREVENTION

Bold statement alert: Western medicine doesn't even know diseases exist until diseases occur.

While prevention has been a catchphrase banted about since the 1950s, as a whole Western medicine has not been very good about *really* integrating prevention into practice. Yes, there's the generic advice about eating right, exercising, and getting enough sleep, but we don't weave this into our medical culture until after a problem starts. And it's a far cry from determining an individual's health risk years down the road. Genetics, epigenetics, and microbiome are at their very early stages in Western medicine. From this perspective, TCM is ahead of the game when it comes to personalizing the gray areas of health and prevention.

Oh sure, the West will ask if you're noshing on processed pork products after your cholesterol rockets out of control, but what mechanisms are in place to help you avoid bacon-sausage-cheese biscuits? Or to motivate you to walk, run, swim, bike, play? Or to maybe not choose phone-scrolling over pillow-hugging at 3 a.m.?

Heck, even if you do receive occasional messages about healthy living as a mode of prevention, something's not working. Despite all of the amazing advances Western medicine has made, we are living in our unhealthiest era—with more heart disease, obesity, and type 2 diabetes than ever before. Make no mistake, that's not Western medicine's *fault*. There are countless contributing factors for why we develop disease. The point is, our culture of practicing prevention needs to be jazzed up.

This is your opportunity to really use Eastern approaches to think about prevention and holistic health. How? With their system, they've developed more sensitive assessments and effective treatments for tipping bodily balance. Here's what you can expect a TCM doctor (we'll show you how to find one on page 251) will do to evaluate your health:

» A physical exam to look for such things as color of your skin and tongue, an examination of your face, and checking your pulse.

» Ask about your occupation to determine what kinds of stressors may be affecting your health.

» Examine your body for muscle tension to see where you're holding your stress.

» Listen to the volume and tone of your voice, because different pitches reflect a different health status.

» Ask specifically what you eat, and perhaps recommend eating less red meat.

» Ask what time you go to bed, as you really should be asleep before 11 p.m. based on TCM circadian rhythm.

» Ask about patterns in menstruation, defecation, and other body functions.

And that's just the start. They'll use many more clues, like a detective, with the goal of helping you achieve bodily balance to maximize your Qi. All of these hints give them subtle details to determine the best paths for *you*.

Can you imagine a primary care doctor going into such depth about these issues in a wellness visit? It just doesn't happen that often, if at all. They may ask if you exercise, or what your diet is like, or if you get enough sleep. They may tell you to cut back on the burgers, bourbon, or banana bread, but it generally won't be a deep-dive into specific life habits.

The point here is, the precision in which Eastern practitioners approach prevention is similar to the precision Western practitioners provide treatment, which is only in its budding stages.

So why wouldn't you want that one-two punch? Reaping the benefits of both approaches. One of the long-standing beliefs of medical practitioners is that prevention is the best form of treatment. Avoid a problem before it even starts. And that's why we're such believers in a possible matrix of medicine between East and West. If you can be more *purposeful* about prevention, you have a much better shot of minimizing your treatments over a lifetime.

TAKE ADVANTAGE OF LOWER COSTS

You don't need us to tell you about the extraordinary cost of Western medicine—whether it comes in the form of insurance deductibles, five-figure hospital bills, monthly prescriptions, or just about anything else health related. In fact, medical expenses are one of the major sources of financial stress for Americans (thus creating a vicious cycle of stress caused by money problems creating more health problems, which create more financial problems—you get the point). Because Western medicine is so advanced for acute and critical care, it's also very expensive and beyond the means of many millions of people around the world.

So why not seize the opportunity to try Eastern techniques for a fraction of what Western treatments cost (whether directly or indirectly)? One of the strengths of Eastern medicine is it's cost effective and can be applied to millions of people in a very efficient way. Herbal medicines (for example, tonics for boosting Qi) are made from widely available, and inexpensive, ingredients.

These formulas have been developed and modified over thousands of years of use. Though there's no Western standard of safety and efficacy testing available for the majority of these tonics, the most common ones are recognized as safe for most people if prescribed correctly. Even if these inexpensive tonics fail for some people, it doesn't leave them broke. The TCM physician will try successively stronger or alternative formulations in an attempt to achieve the desired results. As a first-line attempt at treating certain issues and as a preventative tool, we think TCM techniques are often worth the try.

What Will My Western Docs Think?

Doctors head to medical school thinking that by the end of their training they'll understand all that's worth knowing about the human body and illness—just like we imagined our pediatricians did when they were caring for us as kids. Turns out, this date with destiny never comes.

There's always more to learn and treat, which is part of the joy of medicine. Sometimes the lessons are a topic not mastered in school (pharmacology can be intimidating), or a new discipline is developed (think immunology over the past 25 years). In the case of TCM, an entire new field of practice based on old principles has been rediscovered. After 5,000 years of examination, TCM evokes the wisdom of 1.4 billion people—which is intimidating to any professional who takes pride in their work.

The merger of these leading approaches in worldwide health will take time, so be patient as a patient! Sharing the first few chapters of this book might open your doctor's eyes and ears to a combined method of treatment, or you can introduce a TCM practitioner in your area to your physician. Be the butterfly that fertilizes the different flowers.

APPLY THE HYBRID MODEL TO YOUR LIFE

If you're reading this book, you obviously already have an interest in health and are open to the possibilities of integrating more TCM into your life. So the real challenge isn't about convincing you it's worth a try, but rather figuring out how to best do it.

Now, we should say this: If Western methods are working for you, if they have quieted or cured a problem, and if you have had success, we are *not* suggesting you stop those methods. Remember, it's not "either–or." It's "with."

That said, there are a number of scenarios where taking the hybrid approach is our recommended path. They generally fall into four categories:

If you want to emphasize prevention…For all of the reasons we've outlined above, using TCM gives a structured approach to prevention. Consider TCM if you are at high risk for some diseases, such as having a family history, living in an area with industrial pollution, prone to a sedentary lifestyle, and eating a lot of junk food. Combined with lifestyle choices and mindful changes, TCM approaches can provide an excellent recipe for overall wellness.

If you have a "gray" symptom…The body changes. The body isn't perfect. The body sometimes makes noises, breaks buttons, and churns and gurgles at the most inopportune times. And the body doesn't always work in "A + B = C" equations. If you're experiencing energy or pain issues, hormonal imbalances, or any number of symptoms that make you feel "off," TCM is worth a look.

If Western medicine isn't working for black-and-white issues… We should also be clear that TCM can address very tangible and acute issues, whether it's skin rashes or high blood pressure. If Western solutions have not given you much help, it's worth seeing what Eastern techniques can do in a variety of medical scenarios (this is much of the focus of Part 4).

If you have a DIY philosophy toward medicine… While you certainly need medical professionals for many treatments (nobody's suggesting you dig into that tool chest to use a jigsaw for mole removal), there is a lot you can do on your own. This certainly goes for Western approaches, but for Eastern ones, too. Whether we're talking about herbal remedies or physical methods, if you're the kind of person who likes to take ownership of your body and health, TCM will offer many opportunities for you to do so.

Roadblocks to a Hybrid System

We don't want to imply that we can snap our fingers and change an entire societal approach (we're pushing for nudges in that direction). There are barriers and many complex reasons why it's difficult to integrate the two systems. For example:

» Chinese and Western medicine have different language systems, and the dialogue between them proves to be very difficult (though we hope this book breaks down this barrier).

» There are many phenomena that cannot be explained by modern medicine in the TCM treatment system, and the safety of these measures still needs to be studied.

» Eastern medicine tends to prove success through the comfort and symptoms of the patient, while Western medicine uses laboratory-type diagnostics to determine performance. We lack a unified definition of "success."

PART 2

EASTERN
ESSENTIALS

CHAPTER 4

MINI MED SCHOOL

☯

Understand the three pillars of TCM
to see how it can work for you

When it comes to health and medicine, you're no stranger to the power of a question. How are you feeling? What are your symptoms? What's your family history? Do you really need a dozen sugars for your redwood-sized pumpkin spice latté?

You're used to answering questions, but maybe not this next one—the one that will get us started on a deeper exploration of the foundational medical principles of TCM.

What governs the human body?

A Western medicine reaction to this question may go a little something like this:

Different organs do different things—the brain thinks, the heart moves blood, the kidney filters toxins, the tongue is a squishy landing pad for that latté. Food acts as the power source for all your systems, and—bingo—that's how your body runs.

It's a democratic power structure with each organ and system having domain over their own functions and processes. Occasionally, they converge for a get-together (i.e. the brain sends a calendar invite to the sexual organs for a 10 p.m. "conference"). But typically, they rule their own regions. All of these individual entities collectively oversee this biological society.

If you think this way, you'd certainly be right. That's how our machinery works.

For this chapter, though, we want you to see how another governing system operates—and ultimately why it's okay to think about them as working peacefully together.

In TCM, this society works more like an ecosystem—think about a coral reef or rainforest—where governing principles mix the tangible and intangible. While there are physical elements (just like the rainforest has trees, the body has blood and organs), there's also a bit of art and spirit. When we look at a coral reef, we easily see the dazzling colors and the suppleness of the finger-like tentacles. And we even know from our experience this physical beauty is affected by water temperature, pH, sunlight exposure, etc. However, for an ordinary scuba diver, it takes a leap to see the coral as a living organism by itself. The liveliness within the coral is intangible. Yet it is the miraculous force that creates and maintains the physical beauty, just as Qi to our body.

In that way, there are laws of nature and rhythms of life. There's also a soul that (albeit a bit elusive) is more fundamental than the laws. Knowing the soul allows us to explain the laws. So consider the soul as the law of laws. In TCM, the soul consists of three pillars: Qi, the balance of Yin and Yang, and the Force of Five.

Let's take Yin-Yang as an example. Everything has its Yin side and Yang side, and the two sides must be in balance. For instance, laws govern the heart, brain, and gut: The heart contracts and dilates, brain cells signal through stimulatory and inhibitory neurotransmitters, and the bowel moves its content under the control of sympathetic and parasympathetic nerves. You see here a commonality of these laws, i.e., the biology works by pairs of antagonistic forces. That's the force behind the laws.

While there's the aspect that's all about the machines' parts, nuts, and bolts, there's also value in seeing the body as the coral reef that can only thrive with its bountiful colors and fish when everything is balanced. Here, cycles, patterns, and seasons dictate the overall health of the ecosystem.

Of the two viewpoints above, one isn't better than another—they're just…different. The assembly-line approach works well in some scenarios, but a more nuanced system thrives in others.

Think of this chapter as your crash course in TCM—the medical overview of what governs the human body. Before we launch into the three pillar principles, keep in mind what we said earlier: Allow yourself the head space to explore approaches other than the ones you're accustomed to.

Being treated by mainly Western health professionals your whole life, you surely understand one major unspoken principle that's at the heart of Western med: You have to see it to believe it. You need proof before you act. Proof can come from seeing it physically (like redness of a sore throat or an MRI image of a tumor) or from diagnostic indicators (cholesterol or blood sugar readings). This *tangible* evidence gives you license to act—with surgery, medication, lifestyle interventions, whatever the case may be.

Although this gives us a lot of comfort, Western doctors agree not everything that can be measured is important. And on the flip side, not everything that is important can be measured. For instance, early diagnosis of Alzheimer's disease and cancer are important, but often too elusive for any blood test or radiology exam.

TCM is less governed by see-it-to-believe-it guidelines. It follows a quest to optimize the ecosystem of the body through balance. The body is seen as a functional entity instead of a CT or MRI image. It's a vessel for an experimental model to discover what works for you.

In this chapter, we'll take a closer look at:

HOW the body works: Honoring the *Yin and Yang* philosophy— Yin and Yang is more than just some esoteric or poetic sense of trying to achieve balance, it's a fundamental governing principle: *Everything* has a counterpart.

WHAT governs the body: Unlike the democratic system of organs in Western medicine, TCM lives in an anatomical monarchy. What sits on the throne? *Qi.* Qi is the life force—the building block of the universe—it orchestrates health, wellness, sickness, and bodily efficiencies.

WHEN your body works and *which* decisions to make: The **Force of Five** (a phrase we developed, not TCM's) is sort of like TCM's constitution—the details of how the body should operate. Why five? Virtually everything in TCM is divisible by five. Five also presents as a magic number for interactions bound by a certain set of rules. Sure, Western medicine talks about five fingers, five toes, five extra pounds, but in TCM, you have the five seasons, the five elements, the five Organs, and more. Understanding the Force of Five's overarching message and roles will help you better see how TCM treatments can optimize your health.

So think about it this way: Yin-Yang and Qi are in-the-cloud principles while the Force of Five is more in the weeds—the ins and outs, the tactics, and the operator's manual for the body. Together, the three work in unity to achieve the ultimate goal: making your body a harmonious ecosystem full of life.

Let's see them in action.

YIN AND YANG:
HOW the body works

In Chapter 1, we described Yin-Yang as it relates to a way of thinking—a life and body in balance. And you get the whole dynamic—not just from the popular Yin-Yang image, but because it's something we know from life lessons. We see it in relationships ("you complete me"). We see it spiritually (striving for work-life balance). Heck, we even see it in sandwiches (peanut butter and jelly).

The first medical lesson, though, is that Yin-Yang goes beyond the philosophical. It's an overarching mode of operation for everything that happens in TCM—philosophically, physically, and medically. Derived from Taoist philosophy, the Yin-Yang approach says everything in nature has paradoxical energies that are different but affect each other. And some of these links may seem obvious—interior and exterior of the body, male and female, up and down, hot and cold, dark and light. This concept can be further shown through a tangible example you may have learned when thinking about the human body.

Look at your body's muscular system. It's designed in a Yin-Yang way (even though we don't call it that in Western circles). We have opposing muscles that work in opposite motions—the upper leg has the hamstring in the back and the quadriceps muscle in the front; the upper arm has the biceps muscle in the front and the triceps in the back; the muscles in the chest (which push) oppose the muscles in the back (which pull); and so on.

And here's the thing about the way they work: A body in perfect muscular balance works well and injury-free. But if one area is missing or weaker than another, you cannot stop motion in time. That's when you feel pain and risk injury. The natural idyllic state is to have opposing muscle working *with* each other—even if one is pushing and the other is pulling.

They are opposite, but they must perform together.

This is an easy anatomical way to experience Yin-Yang from a Westernized point of view. The West also describes overall system balance—a state of homeostasis as the body seeks to find even levels.

TCM examines the body much deeper to encompass every organ, every system, every mechanism for operation. Each is divided into two—a Yin-Yang approach to body balance.

- » Yin and Yang are rooted in each other—one cannot exist without the other. For example, you cannot tell north if there's no south.
- » Yin and Yang are like two ends of a seesaw—one side always gains as the other loses. Note this contrasts with some opposing forces that annihilate each other.
- » Ying and Yang take turns to dominate. For instance, the weather takes a turn for the warmer from winter, and a turn for the cooler at the end of summer.

For the West, we hope this creates a foundation of fascination—seeing the opposing, balancing forces that are constantly in flux serving as the umbrella principle for the methods of TCM. Very often, the way problems are diagnosed—even before you feel symptoms—is by recognizing deficiencies or excess in any number of Yin-Yang areas. A breakdown the Yin-Yang balance affects your health status.

In TCM, diseases and illnesses are not viewed as rogue outliers caused from some isolated incident. They often revolve around an imbalance of the almighty Qi.

QI:
WHAT governs the body

In Western medicine, we have nothing quite like Qi. Instead, we break the whole into parts—system, organ, function.

In TCM, Qi is the supreme ruler—the very essence that governs your overall health, wellness, and optimization.

Described as the body's life force, Western populations are eager to write off Qi to its simplest form, quickly assuming it's basically a spirit, soul, or energy—all ethereal concepts that are not easily translated to "real" medicine.

But Qi is much deeper and more powerful than our assumptions. Understanding how it governs wellness lets you see how TCM uses remedies to move Qi around the body and to balance Yin-Yang.

So simply, Qi is the matter and energy that makes up entire universal life forces, as seen here. And because of the TCM principle that the body is the micro universe, your body is made up of Qi as well. As mentioned just a few minutes ago, everything in TCM is divided into Yin and Yang, so it should be no surprise that Qi also has two sides. Yin Qi is the matter that drives down the body's physiological activity (bones, flesh, etc...), while Yang Qi drives up physiological functions via energy flow (blood flow, vital fluid flow, overall energy).

This concept shouldn't be too much of a leap of faith for Western medicine. It's common knowledge that matter consists of energy holding tiny particles together or apart. Ancient Chinese philosophers unified both matter and energy as Qi. In Western medicine, an individual cell is known as the smallest functional unit of the body. It's a small leap to accept that similar cells can be abstracted without regard to their physical boundary to make up the TCM Organs. It's like simply calling digestive function Spleen Qi and reproductive function Kidney Qi. Now take a second leap. TCM believes there's a common denominator of all different types of functions (or Organs), simply referred to as Qi.

The beauty of a unified Qi is, it really is responsible for just about everything in the body. It exists in various shapes and forms:. For instance:

» **Protective Qi**: Responsible for immune function (to defend against invaders)
» **Grain Qi:** Food
» **Natural Qi:** Air
» **Pectoral Qi**: Respiration and blood circulation
» **Nutritive Qi:** Body nourishment
» **Primordial Qi:** Genetics

Qi presents itself in both functional and material forms. It's the body's ability to thrive and work optimally—not just thwart problems, but something more: To be fortified with the power of a diesel engine, the juju of a thousand puppies, the strength of a concrete wall, and the emotional range of an Oscar-winning performer.

Now, we won't get too deep into all the subsets of Qi (there are many, as you just saw), but as we look into the treatment and diagnosis of various problems, it's helpful to see them from a Qi lens.

One important characteristic is its dynamics. Regular motion of Qi around the Organs and other parts of the body is called "Qi movement" (Qi Ji). This movement has four easily understandable directions, Up, Down, In, and Out. For instance, the flow of food in the stomach, hence Stomach Qi, is down. Any problems may lead to nausea and vomiting. Similarly, Lung Qi moves in and out given its breathing motion, and coughing and asthma arise in patients with deficiency. But the movement goes beyond materials. The Spleen Qi moves upward due to its "transform and transport" functions.

There's another incredible form of Qi movement that runs by a "highway system" throughout the body, called meridians (see page 58).

Apart from movement, different Qi are also interconvertible, called "Qi transformation" (Qi Hua). For instance, Primordial Qi (genetics) combined with Grain Qi (food) and Natural Qi (air) form Nutritive Qi and Protective Qi. In essence, Qi transformation is what we call metabolism.

Since Qi takes many shapes and forms, deficiency should widely vary in its manifestations. In clinical practice, TCM typically regards Qi deficiency as Yang Qi deficiency (functional impairment). This deficiency serves as an indicator of suboptimal health in which the Yin-Yang balance starts to jiggle, but often nothing is apparently wrong in lab tests or X-rays. For instance, you can have lack of sleep from Heart Qi deficiency (see Chapter 8), a very defined problem in TCM. Whereas in Western medicine, insomnia is often an elusive diagnosis that's difficult to treat.

THE FORCE OF FIVE:
The WHEN of a body's rhythms and WHICH treatments to use

In basketball, you have a starting five. In music, you groove to the Jackson Five. In happy hours, "it's five o'clock somewhere."

And in TCM, there's what we're calling the Force of Five.

Simply, just as everything is divided into Yin and Yang, almost everything is also divided into parts of five.

The "five" builds the backbone for much of how TCM works, how symptoms are diagnosed, and how illnesses are treated. As is the case with much of this crash course, it's not imperative you recall or remember the specifics of each level of five. It's more important to see the principle in action, which will help you see TCM in action. We won't drill down to every level, but we will hit the major categories.

FIVE ELEMENTS:
Wood, Fire, Earth, Metal, Water

The five elements are part of the infrastructure of the universe, and thus, they are also reflected by five different interrelated movements of the body, energy, and matter. In Eastern terms, they would symbolize various aspects of our health—our emotions, our symptoms, our entire makeup. You may see them as symbolic, but they do have links based in natural phenomena.

» **Wood:** Can be flexed and extended—symbolizes the "free-coursing," "uncluttering," or "break-free" force in the movement of Qi, blood, fluid, etc.

» **Fire:** Flares upward—symbolizes the driving force of blood circulation

» **Earth:** Allows for sowing, growing, and reaping—symbolizes nourishment

» **Metal:** Can be molded and hardened—symbolizes the force of transformation, but evolved to the force that drives dispersing and descending motion

» **Water:** Moistens downward—symbolizes regeneration

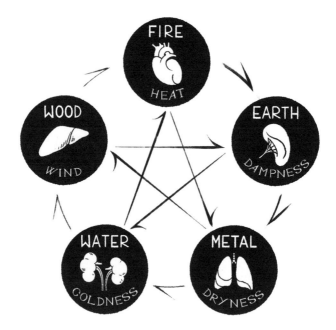

In the Force of Five, there's an intricate relationship among the five we call the law of engendering and restriction. As shown here, the five elements create a cycle, with each element engendering the other (indicated by the circular arrows). And each element also imposes a restricting effect on the one or two elements ahead (indicated by the internal arrows). For instance, Wood engenders Fire, and Water restricts Fire. Both make sense. But fundamentally, the five elements may be understood as a mathematical law, with each element as an algebra symbol.

Since TCM regards humans as the imprint of nature by synchronizing with natural changes, the Force of Five is reflected in humans in a myriad of ways. There are five pathogenic factors, five emotions, five Organs, with the law of engendering and restriction also applying to each.

FIVE PATHOLOGIES:
Wind, Fire/Heat, Dampness, Dryness, Cold

The five pathogenic factors may sound like descriptions of climate to you (which is the point, since nature and the body are connected), but they also represent pathological characteristics.

- » **Wind**: Fast-changing acute conditions—rash, stroke, etc.
- » **Fire/Heat**: Heat-feeling symptoms—fever, pain, flush, bleeding, yellow urine
- » **Dampness**: Stagnation—a full stomach after a meal, a sedentary lifestyle
- » **Cold**: Chill—aversion to cold, cold limbs
- » **Dryness**: Dry feeling in skin—dander and chapping, dry lips, cotton mouth

When these pathologies get a foothold in the body, TCM calls the condition "Excess" as opposed to "Deficiency" derived from the initial jiggle of Yin-Yang balance. Excess is typically the progression of illness from initial imbalance. These pathologies can occur alone, yet in most conditions they are present in combinations. Identifying these pathologies is important in TCM diagnosis and subsequent treatment.

Also note, TCM uses similar terms to describe environmental pathogens, called External Pathogens (or External Evils). There are six External Pathogens: Wind, Fire/Heat, Dampness, Cold, Dryness, and Summer Heat. Each pathogen has its own characteristics, which will be described in later chapters.

FIVE SEASONS:
Spring, Summer, Late Summer, Fall, Winter

Mirroring the seasons of the universe, with Late Summer reflecting the rainy season in central China where the basic philosophy of TCM evolved from farmers. The body's prominence in the universe means efficiencies shouldn't be addressed in an isolated way, but how it may respond to seasons. And these seasons correspond to what you might think of our body's pathology. For instance, Spring is a time of regrowth, whereas Fall is much drier and the season for the pathogen of Dryness. Winter is the season of granary storage and to replenish our body, a good time for tonifying medicinals.

Together, they form a connection—seasons, pathologies, and elements. And this makes sense: The pathology of Fire is associated with anger or redness of the skin, which is symbolically related to the element of Fire and Summer. And the same holds true for pathogens associated with Wind, like sneezing and coughing tied to allergies while connected to the blooming of branches of Spring (where Wood comes in).

FIVE YIN-YANG ORGANS:
Liver and Gallbladder; Heart and Small Intestine; Spleen and Stomach; Lungs and Large Intestines; Kidney and Bladder

An additional Force of Five revolves around Yin-Yang Organs. These Organs are paired with each other. As you already know, in TCM, Organs are not what we traditionally think of in terms of physical characteristics;

the TCM practitioner sees them in terms of function—each Organ/function has a partner.

There are five major Yin-Yang Organs that are paired together and functionally interconnected. Yin Organs (called Zang) have various systematic functions while Yang Organs (called Fu) are all about interfacing with the exterior world. This is where it gets a little confusing for those who grew up with Western medicine. *How in the world do the heart and small intestine go together? The heart pumps blood; the small intestine pumps digested bits of doughnut out the anatomical exit door.*

In TCM, the name of an Organ isn't what you learned in biology class. It's not a mass of tissue that's described by its size, dimension, or makeup. The Kidney isn't a five-inch bean-shaped organ that's located in your belly. The Organs are codes for functions that happen in the body, for instance:

> » **Liver:** Dredger that clears any clog for the running of Qi and other dynamics
> » **Kidney:** Foundation of the body inherited from parents
> » **Stomach:** Holder (a familiar concept if you've ever had one too many scoops of pudding)
> » **Spleen:** Nourisher or transformer that converts food (Essence in TCM) into nutrients
> » **Lung:** Dispenser of sweat and descender of air

Certainly, there are some clear similarities between what you know as the function of the organ and how TCM views them. But the real key is to not see the Organ as a cellular mass, but the uber message describing what your body needs to thrive.

This is precisely the point when the difference between East and West may become clear: West needs a tangible and logical explanation, while TCM uses its long-established dynamic in nature as the lens through which they see the body and how different Organs interconnect each other.

YIN ORGAN (ZANG)		YANG ORGAN (FU)	
Name (nickname)	Function	Name	Transit- Function
Liver (Dredger)	» Store the Blood » De-clog the movement of Qi, Blood, and Fluid	Gallbladder	Bile
Heart (Driver)	» Store the Spirit » Power the Blood movement	Small Intestine	Food
Spleen (Transformer)	» Convert food into nutrients/Essence	Stomach	Food and digestion
Lung (Disperser and Descender)	» Perspiration » Exocrine action, sweating, runny nose » Water metabolism, urination	Large Intestine	Waste
Kidney (Preserver)	» Store Jing (genetic materials) » Water metabolism » Inhalation	Urinary Bladder	Urine

FIVE EMOTIONS/MOODS

Emotion comes in many forms, but TCM characterizes them largely under the Force of Five. TCM also looks at emotion as an indicator of health. Excess emotions lead to Organ-specific injuries:

- » **Anger:** Wood—impacts the Liver
- » **Joy:** Fire—does harm to the Heart
- » **Anxiety:** Earth—affects the Spleen
- » **Sadness:** Metal—burdens the Lung
- » **Fear:** Water—jolts the Kidney

There are two relevant notes to make before we end the story of Force of Five. First, all of these factors play a collective role in the diagnosis of a problem. TCM doctors consider all of them together—the season, the symptoms, the cycles, the physical characteristics of the body orifice, the emotions of the person.

Secondly, as a highly simplified guideline, this theory is to be applied in practice with a certain degree of freedom. While Fire is mainly associated with the Heart, this pathology can often occur to other Organs, and a Heart problem can exhibit other pathologies. TCM doctors work like an environmental field guide—taking in all the clues to determine the best path for treatment.

When looked at in totality, Force of Five gives TCM doctors models for optimal formulas and approaches to address the disruption of balance and restore the body back to its finest natural ecosystem. This lack of rigidity in TCM doctrines is what defines it as the art of medicine.

PUTTING IT ALL TOGETHER

These three governing principles—Yin-Yang, Qi, and the Force of Five—are the architecture for everything that happens in TCM. Together, they answer the big W questions (What, Which, Where, When, with How chirping in). Think of them as the building blocks for a language that defines the state of health and diseases. For instance, "Spleen Qi Deficiency" indicates a condition with Qi (What) in "Spleen (Where), and "Deficiency" tells us to which direction the Yin-Yang balance swings (How). "Cold-Dampness Fettering the Spleen" is a condition in which the Spleen (Where) exhibits pathologies of Cold and Dampness (Which).

Now, as bizarre as the terminologies may seem to be, by understanding the "three-pillar" principles, you may begin to make sense of this language. In fact, this is why we call TCM an "ancient code" in the subtitle of this book, and we made an effort to "biohack" this code with its content.

This ancient code originated from an intuitive association with nature. For instance, Liver is the free-coursing force since it's under Wood. But the code has evolved over time for practical purposes. Both the origin and evolution are so distinct from Western medicine you could liken it to how the peculiar animals in Madagascar evolved on an isolated island. Just as biologists marvel at the unique biology of these animals, biohacking TCM's ancient code would help us gain new insights into medicine.

As described above, this code also exemplifies the balance of function and art. Through basic building blocks TCM gets to the root of an issue, and yet with a certain degree of freedom there's an artistic element and nuance to treatment approaches. It embodies both function and style to create a medical art of healing all its own.

Consider asthma: TCM recognizes asthma as a Lung problem and identifies many causes—one of which is the loss of Yin-Yang balance in the Spleen, resulting in Spleen Qi deficiency. An effective asthma therapy is to use Spleen enhancers, such as the ones we outline on page 124. TCM doctors would find a treatment that considers many factors, including individual seasons and other personal and environmental influences that may come to light during an examination.

Ultimately, this approach of function and art may be one of the roadblocks that holds Western masses back from embracing TCM—if they can't see it, they can't believe it.

But here's the thing: The TCM approach *does* see it. Just maybe not through the lens we're used to.

The Meridian System

The meridian system is the highway of TCM. It's the pathway through which Qi, Blood, and pathogens flow, and it's also the main connector for several TCM treatments, such as acupuncture. The West is familiar with its own body highway systems. Most notably, blood vessels for carrying blood and nutrients and nerves that deliver messages like the Pony Express.

The meridian system is less understood by the West. Not just because it carries Qi, but because of the way it links parts of the body the West doesn't typically associate with one another—like a spot on the foot being connected to headaches. But a foundation of truth is seen when studied by Western medicine. For example, acupuncture needles light up corresponding parts of the brain when they're placed on specific meridians predicted by TCM. The thought is this happens through sensory nerve stimulation that sends signals to the brain, not the classical pathways taught in medical school.

Even with lines clearly depicted on a TCM body surface map, Western researchers have wracked their brain trying to find any physical evidence of meridian. This shouldn't happen to you, though. After reading this chapter, perhaps you've already realized that meridians, like Qi and TCM Organs, are functional instead of physical. In other words, the acupoints that make up the meridians may not have any specific ties to anatomical structure and should not be limited to a physical confine, so long as they affect the Organs in a certain way, be it nervous or hormonal. Nobody has identified any trace of Qi or meridian as part of its moment, or even delineated the boundaries of Organs. Much like an elusive photon under the rule of wave-particle duality, they could be lurking anywhere in the body.

Windows to Your Health

To get a sense of how TCM pictures the inter-connections of your body, let's start simple.

Ears: Your ears connect to various Organs in your body through a variety of meridians. Applying pressure or massage to specific points can help a variety of problems. For example, gently massaging your lobes can relieve headaches or eye strain. Rubbing the notch near the entrance of the ear canal can help improve blood flow. And stimulating the inner ridge of the ear can help reduce stress or pain in your back, shoulders, and neck.

Lips: Pale lips indicate a lack of Qi, Blood, and nutrients, while deep-red and dry lips show there's too much Heat. Cracked lips signal your Spleen and Stomach need more fluids, while sore or chapped lips suggest Dryness and Heat, and purplish lips suggest Blood stasis.

Tongue: The color of your tongue changes based on your overall health. And the regions of your tongue correspond to various TCM Organs. A normal tongue is pink, so if your tongue is pale, it indicates you're deficient in Blood Qi and may feel lethargic. A dark red tongue indicates excess Heat, which manifests itself in anxiety or insomnia. Also look out for coatings on your tongue which can signal a variety of issues going on inside your body. For example, a thick and greasy coating can indicate you're having poor digestion and may experience weight gain or lethargy. An ideal coating is thin and white.

Eyes: Your eyes also reveal something about what is happening inside your body. Puffy eyes show a deficiency in Spleen, and red eyes may suggest Liver Fire.

Stagnation: The Enemy of Health

We all know that stagnation isn't good when it comes to rivers, careers, romantic relationships, or cottage cheese. Same's true for our bodies.

Our bodies work best when our energy—and all of the blood, fluid, and systems—are humming along. When they move like rivers (rather than fester like a puddle), we are at our strongest. One of TCM's goals is to avoid biological stagnation and create bodies that move with strong flow, motion, and life rhythms.

What happens under stagnation? There are many scenarios. If Spirit (the TCM term for mental activities) is restrained, depression occurs. If Spleen (digestive function) slows down, constipation occurs, often accompanied by abdominal pain. All kinds of pain follow stagnation. The TCM doctrine goes: Where there's pain, there's impediment. Joint pain, neck and shoulder pain, and muscle pain are attributed to what's called blockade syndrome—a sore throat is associated with throat blockade.

Given stagnation is a common denominator in many illnesses, TCM identifies stagnation as a pathological factor in its own right. It even believes there is a special force in the body—the TCM Organ Liver—that fights against it. Liver is compared to a "dredger"; it clears the runway of Qi, Blood, and body fluids. As we explain, TCM Organ function is not conceptualized by anatomical locations. This perspective is unique, one that has caused some of the confusion for Westerners learning more about Eastern medicine.

So what causes stagnation? It starts at the Liver. When the dredger's function is lost, Liver Qi stagnation (a term you'll encounter many times in this book) occurs. Other causes stem from TCM's version of pathogens, i.e., "evils" (Wind, Cold, Fire/Hot, Damp, Dry). While all five have a prominent place in TCM, let's look at the one related to stagnation in particular, Dampness.

At first, you might chalk Dampness up as a concept that's too vague or simply symbolic. What the heck does it mean?

The essence of Dampness as an evil coincides with the concept of a waterlogged body in which the energy of life force (Qi) is stagnant and cannot move around the body smoothly. After Dampness invades the body, circulation of fluids and systems stall, creating congestion and causing regional dysfunction of life systems, such as immune, circulatory, and digestive systems.

CHAPTER 5

THE TRICKS OF
TCM TRIAGE

☯

How TCM diagnoses and treats problems
differently for different people

Remember when making coffee meant, well, making a pot of coffee? No fuss, no decisions, no choices. Turn the pot on, brew, drink.

Today, you walk into a coffee shop and you have limitless options. Different sizes, different flavors, different concoctions, two pumps of this, three shots of that, with foam, without foam, almond milk, coconut milk, extra wet on the cappuccino, super light on the syrup, "you're darn right I'd like whipped cream," on and on.

You get what you want in whatever way you want.

When it comes to treatment options for health and wellness, the TCM doctor is a bit like a modern-day barista. The job? Think about a variety of factors and options to concoct exactly what's right for *you*. While it's not like you'll order up a "venti astragalus latté with extra Qi," the point is this: customization and personalization is key.

Western medicine tends to have standard courses of treatment: X prescription for Y infection, X surgery for Y malfunction, X cream for Y itchy parts.

TCM doesn't work this way. Its algebraic equations are a bit more artistic, considering not just X and Y, but all the factors that determine what is really causing X and which Y might be best. This is where the concept of "degree of freedom" in mathematics fully applies.

For many Westerners, this concept isn't easy to grasp. After all, why shouldn't there be the same treatment for the same problem? It all goes back to the root principles of TCM. A body seeking balance can be thrown off for any number of reasons, including time of day, climate, personal biology, and on and on. So to have only one treatment for one issue feels more like a factory setting than a personalized approach.

It's the difference between getting the convention-brewed coffee from a two-gallon dispenser and ordering your own grandé caramel macchiato with two shots of espresso.

Before we touch on specific ailments and pathologies, we'll spend some time giving you an overview of the TCM approach to diagnosing problems and treating them. You'll see these and more throughout the rest of the book. This baseline understanding will help you see how TCM works in action, no matter whether we're talking about fatigue or diarrhea, pain or asthma, heart troubles or sexual dysfunction.

The standard principle for treatment revolves around the ethics of humanity—that each TCM practitioner takes the time and diligence to work through the art of healing.

HOW TCM DOCTORS MAKE A DIAGNOSIS

TCM doctors don't have a lab. They don't take blood samples to study under a microscope and run through a machine to reveal all sorts of numbers. They don't order X-rays, CTs, MRIs, or ultrasounds to see what's going wrong inside the body. They don't even hook up an ECG to see if a patient is having a heart attack. Surprisingly, they don't even use a stethoscope. So how is it possible for TCM doctors to get the right diagnosis and make sure a patient has the best possible treatment? What's the magic?

Let's take one of the most common TCM conditions, Qi Deficiency, for a spin. Here's how a typical TCM diagnosis looks:

As the patient enters the room, the first sight of his body language gives him away as a lethargic. Next, he'll mutter "I feel so tired" in a low voice. A deeper look reveals a pale face and a large tongue with tooth marks on both sides.

The doctor starts to suspect a Qi deficiency and subsequently asks a number of questions to confirm if the patient often feels short of breath, tends to sweat without strenuous physical activity, and if he readily gets a cold or flu. Finally, the doctor will feel his pulse. A weak pulse would clinch the diagnosis of Qi deficiency.

You see here, the diagnostics of TCM largely consist of the following four techniques (Four Assessments). Each provides a unique understanding of health.

> » **Visual inspection.** Examination of the physique, face, and especially the tongue. There's a ton of telltale signs that can be revealed from the tongue. For instance, a voluminous tongue with teeth marks on the sides and white fur on top indicates Qi deficiency.

> » **Voice and smell.** The voice and sometimes the smell of patients tell a lot about them. Patients with Qi deficiency often speak with low voices.

> » **Questions.** Doctors learn the symptoms through the patient's responses to their questions. For instance, aversion to cold suggests Yang deficiency; and frequent night urination, in particular, suggests Kidney Yang Deficiency.

> » **Palpation or pulse-feeling.** Remarkably, TCM doctors are able to distinguish dozens of pulse patterns that correspond to

different pathology. For example, the pulse that feels like touch-
ing the strings of a violin, called wiry pulse, indicates problems
with liver, gallbladder, and sometimes chronic pain.

So there's a symptom pattern, tongue pattern, and pulse pattern, and
so on. TCM names different facets of the diagnosis "Xiang" or pattern.
Different patterns combine to make up a "Zheng" or syndrome. Syndrome
diagnosis is a very different concept from that of Western medicine. A
Western syndrome is simply a group of symptoms that often occur
together in patients, like irritable bowel syndrome, with no indication of
any underlying pathology.

In contrast, TCM syndrome is a vital part of the TCM diagnostic
process called syndrome differentiation. Syndrome differentiation ana-
lyzes the information obtained from the diagnosis in the context of TCM
principles (Yin-Yang, Qi, and the Force of Five). In a word, it's a processor
that speedily converts input data (from Four Assessments) to output a
comprehensive diagnosis.

Or to put it another way, Western medicine would diagnose whether a
car is running or not, while TCM would listen to the hum of the engine—
hear how smooth it sounds, the way it purrs—and assess overall health
to optimize the car's performance.

That's why a TCM diagnosis is often instant. One visit to the TCM
clinic usually does it. You don't see patients running around different labs,
let alone sometimes going weeks or months with a FUO (fever of unknown
origin) on their medical records.

It makes sense that TCM doesn't depend upon radiology and biochemistry assessments. The key is holism. Recall that TCM Organs are
functional instead of physical or anatomical. Therefore, the utility of a CT,
MRI, or biopsy that pinpoints an illness is limited in TCM practice. So are
biochemistry markers where each reflects one aspect of metabolism that
may go awry. This brings up another fundamental of Chinese diagnosis:
"A part reflects the whole." Pathology of the whole body can be reflected
in a specific part of the body, and illness in the internal Organs can be

reflected in the corresponding exterior. For example, dryness of the eyes usually indicates deficiency of Liver-Yin or Liver-Blood. The seemingly "crude" TCM diagnostics are well suited for its purpose.

This is not to say, however, that more sophisticated Western tests have no place in TCM. As we consider what a hybrid system could look like, wouldn't it be game changing to come up with a diagnostic marker to measure your Qi? And given Eastern medicine diagnoses imbalance through sight, physical exams, and symptoms, would Western culture be open to a Qi score? Together, is there a way to tangibly show if you have excess or deficiency to seek options for treatment? Will this ever happen? Hard to say. But it's a provocative thought to dream of a time when your blood panel could be labeled with such things as HDL, LDL, IgA, B12, and Qi. Indeed, studies are investigating novel biomarkers to add to the existing measures of Four Assessments. If a look of the tongue reveals Qi deficiency, how about an X-ray of the chest? Could a test of amylase in the saliva be an indicator of Spleen Qi?

Another important field of TCM diagnostic research is to standardize the Four Assessments to achieve a consistent diagnosis. For instance, exactly how low a voice is required for Qi deficiency? This level of standardization is something researchers already have in mind. Standardizing TCM diagnosis has been widely studied in recent decades in China. Professor Wang at Beijing University of Chinese Medicine is one example. With thousands of patients of Qi deficiency, he was able to assemble a Qi score from a number of Qi-relevant symptoms (the same rationale used for the quiz you took at the beginning of the book). This score creates an index to gauge your Qi level, similar to a lab report of your blood sugar. Clearly defined criteria not only helps the accuracy of diagnosis, it also paves the way for clinical trials to stringently test TCM therapies.

HEALTH IS ABOUT GETTING AHEAD OF THE ISSUES

Make no mistake: We're in a crisis when it comes to chronic disease. Diabetes, heart disease, inflammation, and so much more. And it's literally killing millions of us. Western medicine has a handle on various advancements and treatments (many of which work extremely well). But with no concrete way to measure and contain the fast-rising number of chronic diseases, it's worth looking into time-honored TCM therapies to help fight off and fix chronic conditions. In fact, TCM has done very well in comparison with Western medicine to treat these chronic killers.

As you know, chronic issues are traditionally a tough beast to tame. Often, this means lifelong medications or learning to tolerate lifelong symptoms and problems. We explore chronic conditions throughout *Yin Yang You*, but the common biology for many of them comes down to this: Some kind of system error has taken place inside your bodily universe. This error then becomes a part of your cycle and feedback loop as your body continues to operate with this error. The overall function of your body is impaired, ultimately leading to the degradation of life force and disease.

Take chronic inflammation: it's when your immune system overreacts to a problem and essentially can't shut off in a timely way. Thus causing a whole host of reactionary problems as your body stays in a constant fighting state. Chronic inflammation is difficult to quiet (though it can be done through lifestyle and medical treatments) unless you get to the root cause of the trigger and reaction (something Western medicine is not always very good at).

Why is TCM good at fighting chronic issues?

First of all, chronic issues come with an elusive slow start. There's a sub-clinical stage that doesn't show symptoms. It's essentially when your Yin and Yang balance starts to sway to one direction but is yet to pass a tipping point. It's where the TCM pathology of deficiency starts to show up. That's why TCM excels in prevention, because it has a clear concept and the ways and means of dealing with it—tonifying medicinals for rectifying the deficiency, for instance.

Second, deficiency invites evils. As the doctrine goes: Where Righteous (Normal) Qi exists, evils gain no entry. Further progression of deficiency leads to invasion of the pathogens. This is typically the stage symptoms start to show. A strong example of this is Spleen-Dampness. Unhealthy diets like fats and sweets impair Spleen, cause Spleen deficiency, which in turn brings Dampness.

This pathology is repeated many times with common chronic problems. It's important to see the correlations, and just as interesting, the contrast in how TCM and Western medicine views the genesis and progression of chronic diseases.

Western → **HEALTHY**   **BALANCED** ← Eastern

Western → **SUBCLINICAL**   **DEFICIENT** ← Eastern
(*early stages of a problem*)

Western → **CLINICAL**   **EXCESS** ← Eastern
(*Pathogenic Invasion*)

The emphasis for TCM doctors is to look at the body as a whole, see where there may be deficiencies *and* excess (pathogen or "Evils"), and if the issue is at its early stage, the priority is to restore balance before any problems surface. As such, there tends to be a much greater emphasis on building wellness as a part of the fabric of daily living to avoid major problems down the road. It's less reactionary and more prevention-oriented. This doesn't mean problems don't have solutions, the focus is simply to avoid the problem in the first place—optimizing the body for healthy, balanced, energized living.

In addition to the Yin-Yang thinking, TCM also has an edge in fighting chronic diseases from its holistic approach. Let's make headache as an example here. Headache is often attributed by the holistic process (syndrome differentiation) to "flaming-up of the Liver Yang" (a condition resembling hypertension caused headache). This syndrome is in turn initiated by Liver Qi stagnation, a well-recognized condition that can be treated effectively with TCM "Qi-smoothening" medicinals. You see here TCM gets to the root of the symptom, which helps to stop it from sprouting into a complex and lingering problem.

THE MAIN PRINCIPLES OF TREATMENT

Before we jump to the kinds of approaches TCM docs take, it makes sense to talk through the main ways they perceive treatment. That's because their "why we do it" reasons inform their "what we do" actions. The main guiding philosophies include:

» **Prevention of disease leads; treatment of disease follows.** While Western medicine often seems to be either preventative or treatment focused, TCM often looks at balancing both at the same time—treating a complaint and preventing its future manifestations. These, of course, are more subtle nudges toward wellness (there's no TCM version of open heart surgery).

» **Personalization matters most.** When the West talks about personalized medicine, you may think about family genetic history and the like. TCM practitioners not only think about how each individual is evaluated, but also consider such things as environmental factors. The season, time of day, and many other personal circumstances, like emotional status, that can influence the balance of the body are surveyed. These factors are all embedded in the Force of Five matrix described in the Mini Med School chapter.

» **Treatment ends with the same goal.** In the West, we may think about erasing the rash, eliminating the pain, or clearing out the mucus. In the East, the ultimate goal revolves around restoring Qi to a free flow so the rash and pain will naturally disappear. That means exploring whether there's a deficiency or excess and tinkering with treatments to help find total-body Yin-Yang balance. And it's why TCM solutions are so variable and subtle. There's an art to the treatment—restoring balance and finding whole-body wellness and optimization.

THE MAIN METHODS OF TREATMENT

The metaphorical medicine cabinet in the West looks a little something like this: surgery, medication, lifestyle choices. The same medicine cabinet in the East looks similar upon first glance, but the differences are in the details. TCM doctors will use any or all kinds of methods in the hope of restoring balance. The major approaches incorporate:

HERBAL REMEDIES: It's not surprising that TCM's philosophy and healing stem from nature and the union between the body and elements. TCM drugs come from herbs, minerals, even animal tissues. But the mainstem treatment is herbal—plant-based compounds used for medicinal purposes. As you might suspect, there are thousands of different herbals, which is why the barista approach makes so much sense.

The discovery and use of medicinal plants started with Shennong, the Chinese god of agriculture. This deity tasted plants and water in various places to test the effects on the body. The legend of Shennong sampling hundreds of plants a day depicts how the ancient herbals effects on the body were revealed. They found mint leaves cooling and comforting to the throat, ginger helped soothe the stomach, rhubarbs eased constipation, and so much more. Over time, people learned what to eat when and what shouldn't, and couldn't, be eaten.

Often herbals are used in combination (formula). The combination depends on multiple factors, like personal balance, time, seasons, and so on. In fact, the herbal formula usually contains a primary ingredient (the King in government parlance), a secondary one (the Minister), one to counter side effects (the Assistant), and one to enhance GI absorption (the Envoy).

You'll learn about many of these as you move through the rest of the book, but it's interesting to note that herbs account for the largest proportion of all medicinal plants.

TCM doctors roughly use 365 main herbs (symbolic of one for each day) to treat most problems. And they're used in a variety of ways and combinations based on the person and the syndrome.

These medicinals help restore inner balance and are generally divided up by two aspects:

1. **They are categorized by five thermal properties of Heat, Warm, Neutral, Cool, and Cold**—each relevant to treat the TCM pathogens of Fire (or Heat) and Cold.
2. **They refer to the five tastes of sour, bitter, sweet, spicy, and salty**—each corresponds to and has therapeutic effect for one of the five TCM Organs.

Throughout the last half of the book, you will see these in action—the seed of feather cockscomb clearing away Liver Fire and brightening the eyes, or cinnamon bark relieving the Cold and warming the Stomach and Kidney.

A big concern about herbal therapies lies with the interactions of TCM and Western drugs when you start playing chemistry lab inside your body. All drugs are tested by themselves, but not much is known about what will happen if you take six Western and TCM drugs simultaneously. Always let your caregivers know all the herbal and prescribed supplements and medications you are taking so they can monitor them closely. Plus, they may learn from your experience and recommend duplicating your approach to future patients with similar problems.

DIETARY APPROACHES: Like much of the West, the East also believes that food has an incredible power to heal (though they've known it for much longer). Food—the kind that comes from nature, not from a plastic bag—has positive effects on the body. We'll talk about food therapy at length in the next chapter. You will see that TCM has in-depth knowledge of food, its own version of nutritional science.

Overall, a TCM diet tends to revolve around food that has tonic properties and is good for prevention purposes. These tonics are normally safe to use every day. Don't think of dietary supplements like vitamin C and zinc pills, but instead actual food. And it's delicious! Chinese yam is a wonderful example of a healing food to cook and serve as a meal.

But East and West speak about the power of food differently. In the West, we tend to simplify foods, talking about them as completely healthy or absolutely bad. Vegetables are good. Puffy snacks with orange-cheese that stays on your fingers for 14 hours, not so much. The TCM approach not only considers the food itself, but also how it interacts with the universe. TCM's food philosophy says "eat turnips in the winter and ginger in the summer," acknowledging there's a seasonal effect on how food interacts with your body. And that aforementioned ginger? It's helpful in the morning to warm the stomach and intestines, but harmful in the evening, with a spear-like effect that time of day.

QI GONG: Qi Gong literally means the skill of enhancing the flow of Qi and Blood. It's a common practice in TCM therapy and has multiple techniques—all to improve bodily function by adjusting one's mental state, movement, and breathing. Among these three, mental state is the most important. The other two are ways and means to improve one's mental state. Recall what we said about Five Emotions in Chapter 4. These emotions have a direct impact on health. Similarly, Qi Gong seeks to control mental activity to improve the state of Qi and Blood.

It's clear motion and breathing are related to mental state. You take a deep breath when you are in for a big shock. The parts of the brain that control breathing and motion also connect to your emotions. Qi Gong takes control of these connections for health benefits. From this point of view, Qi Gong is very different from physical exercise, although to an outsider's eyes the two may look similar.

Qi Gong has developed into various techniques. Static Qi Gong looks like Yoga or Buddhism meditation, whereas dynamic Qi Gong uses bodily movement. One type (Wu Qing Xi, or Five Animal Game) imitates the movements and expressions of five animals—bear, tiger, ape, deer, and bird. Another type (Ba Duan Jin) is composed of eight actions, each suitable for the health and care of corresponding Organs. Routines may be prescribed based on evaluation of a person and customized based on Organs, diseases, and deficiencies.

In the West, we've seen a much greater emphasis on things like mobility—not just strengthening muscles or burning fat, but improving the body's ability to work along different planes of motion. This is a benefit of Qi Gong as you progress through its various positions.

» **Crossed Leg Sitting:** The back of feet can touch the ground or rest on the thigh of the opposing leg. This is the most basic posture for Qi Gong.

» **GuanYuan Acupoint:** Concentrate the thoughts on the area four fingers below the navel and breathe gently and rhythmically.

Qi Gong is commonly used in treating depression, fatigue, pain, and is even used in cosmetics.

TAI CHI: Tai chi originated as a martial art hundreds of years ago. It's rooted in the Chinese Yin-Yang philosophy. The knack is to avoid resisting the brute attacking force of the opponent (Yang), but to meet it in softness (Yin) and redirect it to exhaustion. Over time, a gentler version of Tai Chi morphed into a health care exercise. This discipline incorporates some elements of Qi Gong, particularly controlling Qi movement, but the focus is more on the development of strength.

Think of a weightlifter building up his arms with biceps curls. The weightlifter repeats curls to build muscle, focusing on that muscle only. In the same way, Qi Gong focuses on a particular issue in the mind, body, or spirit. Tai Chi is more like a full-body weightlifting routine that typically involves more complex, choreographed postures. It has been shown to reduce pain in a variety of diseases, along with other benefits such as reducing anxiety.

ACUPUNCTURE: You may know it as the needle-in-the-skin treatment. And you may have heard a needle in the foot or a squeeze in the hand can help with headaches. Yes, it's true, this method uses small needles inserted into the body to engage the meridian principles. As you may remember, meridians are channels of Qi that run throughout and energetically connect internal Organs with other parts of the body. A needle inserted into channels and maneuvered by different hand skills is able to modulate the Qi state in the Organs, be it Qi deficiency or stagnation. Acupuncture is shown to be effective in reducing post-operative pain, nausea during pregnancy, nausea and vomiting caused by chemotherapy, and toothache with minimal side effects.

The reason behind this head-scratching phenomenon remains largely unclear. Researchers have found acupuncture on acupoints like Hugu (well-known for a squeeze on hand to relieve pain) may increase blood endorphin, a hormone that works similar to morphine for pain relief. So there might be some scientific explanation, but there's surely a long way to go for scientists.

Fun fact: The predecessor to the acupuncture needle was called the Bian-stone—a wedge stone or small cone made by grinding a stone and used to alleviate pain. When metallurgy was invented, needle instruments were developed and improved over time, differing in shape and function based on the kind of treatment.

TUINA (ACUPRESSURE AND MASSAGE): TuiNa is a TCM therapy that utilizes various hand and elbow techniques to improve Qi and Blood flow by stimulating the surface of the body or acupoints. This may include exerting pressure (acupressure) on acupoints using the same rationale as acupuncture. But often other techniques are also often used—rubbing, pushing, grasping, kneading, chafing, pinching, patting, and more. Some of the TuiNa maneuvers are simple and the acupoints are easy to locate, so they can be used as do-it-yourself TCM treatments. In later chapters of *Yin Yang You*, you'll be introduced to self-massage for treating various conditions.

Try it yourself. Locate the acupressure point on your hand, the thenar branch of the median nerve located between your thumb and index finger (see right). Massage for five minutes to lower cortisol levels and release the stress-reducing hormone oxytocin.

MOXIBUSTION: A form of heat therapy where leaves of the moxa plant are burned in proximity to the surface of the skin, often over an acupoint. Like acupuncture, moxibustion works to clear and open meridians blocked by disease. The point is to not only destroy pathogen, but also to open up Qi pathways. This is especially helpful for menstrual cramps and premenstrual syndrome (PMS).

This therapy developed after people learned how to use fire. They began lighting various branches to fight ailments associated with the Cold pathogen, as you might expect.

While performing moxibustion with the moxa stick, first tear apart the packing paper at one end, then light the moxa stick and keep the lit end right over the selected acupuncture point at a proper distance so you can assess the temperature immediately. Place the index and the middle fingers of one hand on the two sides of the acupuncture point to feel the temperature. Children and the elderly can be easily scalded, so it's best they have the help of another person to perform moxibustion.

The moxibustion box can be used on flat parts such as the belly and back. Put an appropriate length of lighted moxa stick into the moxibustion box and place the box on the acupuncture point. When you feel heat, it's time to replace the moxa cone with a new one. To prevent scalding or to strengthen the effect of moxibustion, salt, a ginger or garlic slice, or other medicines can be placed between the moxa cone and the skin.

CUPPING: You may be most familiar with cupping when you saw the red circles on Michael Phelps' back during the Olympics. Cupping therapy dates back more than 2,000 years in TCM. It was called "horn cupping" in ancient China. Why? People would empty the horn of cattle or sheep and grind it into a cone with a hole. They'd then repeatedly use it to stimulate an abscess, after which they'd pierce through the abscess to extract the puss-containing blood with the hollowed horn. This might be the earliest cupping therapy.

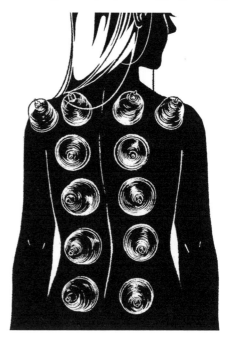

Today's cupping therapy is vastly different. It uses various cups as the tool. A negative pressure is formed by burning the air inside the cup so it can be suctioned on the body's surface. Temperature stimulates the skin and causes dermohemia to expel Cold and clear

Dampness, promote the flow of Qi and Blood circulation, draw out poison and purging Heat, and regulate Yin and Yang.

AURICULAR THERAPY (EAR SEED PRESSURE AND EAR ACU-PUNCTURE): Ear seeds are small seeds that can be placed on your ear with adhesive; the seeds are then pressed by hand to stimulate the acupoints to improve or treat various health problems. It's another type of acupuncture. The concept originates from TCM's viewing a part of body as a microcosm of the whole, similar to the idea that "the universe imprints the human body." In auricular therapy, many body ailments are reflected on the ears via acupoints, and maneuvers on these acupoints are designed to specifically care for each. This therapy is effective to treat addictions, neurasthenia, toothache etc. While you can apply them yourself, a TCM doc or acupuncturist can help direct you for the best placement, according to the principle in which a specific position on the ear corresponds to a specific Organ.

CHRONOTHERAPY: One of the ways TCM is very different from Western medicine is it places a much heavier emphasis on time and the role it plays in our health. Our bodies—in relationship with the ebb and flow of every day—are meant to do certain things at certain times. The TCM circadian clock works in two 12-hour chunks, with each chunk consisting of six 2-hour intervals. Each interval corresponds to the timing of peak activity of each TCM Organ, indicating the optimal time for engagement. Our bodies

function best when respecting the rhythms of the universe. This is how it looks:

5:00–7:00 A.M.	Large intestine meridian—drink water and exercise
7:00–9:00 A.M.	Stomach meridian—eat breakfast
9:00–11:00 A.M.	Spleen meridian—engage in mental activities
11:00 A.M.–1:00 P.M.	Heart meridian—take a nap
1:00–3:00 P.M.	Small intestine meridian—sip a cup of tea
3:00–5:00 P.M.	Bladder meridian—learn and work
5:00–7:00 P.M.	Kidney meridian—nourish Essence
7:00–9:00 PM.	Pericardium meridian—walk and prepare for sleep
9:00–11:00 P.M.	Triple energizer meridian—soak feet in warm water
11:00 P.M.–1:00 A.M.	Gallbladder meridian—sleep
1:00–3:00 A.M.	Liver meridian—don't drink or stay up late
3:00–5:00 A.M.	Lung meridian—sleep deeply

AROMATHERAPY: We should note that aromatherapy is not generally considered a TCM approach, but there are similar principles when it comes to the use of herbals in treatments.

Essential oils are compounds extracted from plants that contain the essence of the plant's make up—scents and other healing compounds that may be absorbed through the skin. They are believed to work by infusing into the bloodstream to effect Qi and influence your mind and hormones. Oils are either Yin, Yang, or neutral. As you would expect, Yin oils enhance the Yin side of the body and Yang oils work on the Yang side.

Yin: Florals like chamomile, lavender, rose, geranium. Citrus like bergamot, grapefruit, lemon. Cooling like peppermint and spearmint.

Yang: Spicy like cardamom, cinnamon, ginger. Herbaceous like rosemary and thyme.

Neutral: Orange, sage.

Yin or Yang: Woody

As is the case with all treatments, aromatherapy is developed based on a number of factors—including the ailment and the person in terms of their mood, energy, sleep patterns, stress levels, aroma preferences, and more. Western medicine has aromatherapy as well. It uses scents like chamomile and lavender to relieve anxiety and insomnia. Some clinical studies provide support for the aromatherapy approach.

The Five Sounds of TCM

Music is considered one of the great healers of TCM. The tones of healing follow the same tones you may be familiar with—do, re, mi, so, and la. A great emphasis is placed on using music as part of the healing process.

GONG–DO: Peaceful and steady—it empowers Spleen and helps with digestion, metabolism, and energy.

SHANG–RE: Harmonious and nurturing—it empowers the Lungs, which helps with breathing, skin, and the body's defenses.

JUE–MI: Youthful and uplifting—it empowers the Liver, which helps with digestion, mood, and sleep.

ZHI–SO: Passionate and joyful—it empowers the Heart, which helps with mood, circulatory issues, and cognition.

YU–LA: Powerful and purifying—it empowers the Kidneys, which helps with hearing and sexual function.

CHAPTER 6

YIN YANG YUM

Rebalance your food therapy approach with kitchen wisdom to better optimize your health and your body

You're no stranger to complicated relationships. While you may have complex emotional tangos with in-laws, bosses, or that lovely lipped ex who just sent you a friend request (#TwelveYearsLater), you've probably also wrestled with another big character in your life: Food.

For many of us with health issues, there may not be a more dubious connection than the one you have with eating and drinking. On one hand, meals can give you so much joy—bringing back memories of family dinners, aromatic kitchens, celebratory clinks of glasses, holiday cheer, and especially mama's killer meatballs in marinara.

Yet at the same time, food can be suspect number one when it comes to high blood test numbers, the one on the scale—busted waistbands and broken dreams—and the reason why you sometimes feel you move through life more like a manatee than a manta ray.

What started as delight (perfect pepperoni pleasure!) ended up as destruction (your very own Stromboli-belly!).

The U.S. certainly has struggled with issues related to overeating; everything from heart disease and diabetes to some cancers and dementia have links to obesity and being overweight. Our eating issues are thorny. They can involve genetic, environmental, behavioral, socioeconomic, and other factors. For that reason, we're not going to break down every food-related challenge you may have.

Instead, we want to look at how TCM views eating, ingredients, meals, and our relationship with food. In some ways, it's very different from how Western people think. In others, it's quite similar. Our hope is you'll take some of the major principles and lessons and apply them to your life, keeping this main maxim in mind:

- » Food has the power to heal.
- » Food has the power to energize you.
- » Food can be your greatest tool to improve the way you function and how you feel.

According to TCM, diseases come through the mouth, suggesting that what you eat plays a role in health and disease. Let's look at TCM's leading food philosophies.

THINK SENSATION MORE SO THAN NUTRITION

Simply put, we see food as pleasure (a giant chicken parm sandwich of holy goodness that needs to find a loving home down the way from Esophagus Avenue), and coming in close second, for its nutrition—fat, carbs, protein, vitamins, minerals, calories. Food is thought of both scientifically and chemically—how it works in the body, gets shuttled through the bloodstream, powers our organs, can get stored as fat, and so on.

It's not uncommon for food to be compared to fuel, because that's the function of food—it provides the energy to make our system go. That's the way a lot of us think. Food is like the gas in a car. Some fuel is higher quality than others, and some is crappy. Use the best kind for the best performance. Fill up with sub-standard quality and you'll turn into a slumping heap of fleshy goo.

Very nutritional, very precise, very scientific.

Very different from the way TCM thinks about a solid meal.

TCM sees the energy in food, but also looks at the synchronicity and artistry of non-structural attributes, like its temperature or the time you eat it.

While Western science has broken down food by nutrients and chemicals, TCM foods are classified by flavors (sour, sweet, bitter, spicy, and salty) and thermal properties (the effect on the body such as making you feel cold, cool, neutral, warm, hot). Of course, the five flavors go much deeper than the sensation of the taste buds. Each flavor reflects one of the multifaceted Force of Five, the workings (When and Where) of the cosmos our body. They crosstalk with other facets. Like the seasons, Organs and pathologies, impact our health, thus adding a whole layer of sophistication to dietary therapy. So do thermal properties. Hot foods fight against the pathology of Cold, and cold food against that of Heat.

If the West thinks of food as fuel for a car, TCM thinks of food more like the elements that help plants grow. For plants to thrive, they need sun and rain in the right balance to weather the elements of the season. You don't want too much or too little of sun or rain, just a nice, healthy dose of both. Follow the laws of nature and the universe and the ecosystem keeps running. The sun and rain are the food, of course, while the plant is the human body.

So there's just a little more elegance and a lot less nutritional focus in this approach to eating (TCM doesn't even use the word nutrition, but rather "food therapy").

Ultimately, TCM views the body as its own greatest healer—it can right its own ship when in proper balance. And food is one of the main ways to do this.

It strikes us how blending these methods would better our relationship with food to improve our bodies. Both cultures see food as helping us achieve the ultimate goal—living longer, youthful, and more active lives. TCM just thinks about it a bit differently. They look to food for improving four main areas: Qi, Blood, bodily fluids, and body Essence.

Healthy eating replenishes vital energy, helps achieve Yin and Yang balance, and prevents disease.

THE BAROMETER OF BALANCE

Eat a balanced diet. You've heard the phrase all your life. Maybe as a kid this meant your plate had chicken, rice, and a salad. And in college perhaps your idea of a balanced diet was Froot Loops and beer. The notion of "balance" has many variations in Western diets, but the general concept is the same: Diversify your food choices to make sure you're getting essential macronutrients and micronutrients to feed and fuel your body. Now what those combos look like depend on the diet or eating plan (some modern-day diets, like keto, actually advocate for limiting or severely restricting a food group or macronutrient).

In TCM, the idea of balance unsurprisingly reigns supreme. While practitioners don't measure out foods or divide up the exact ratios of nutrition, the whole idea is eating should be diversified for optimum body support.

What may be surprising is this idea of balance extends far beyond specific foods, using TCM's unique characterization of foods.

FORCE OF FIVE: In order of importance, the food groups in TCM are grains (the bottom of a food pyramid), then animal meat, then vegetables, and finally fruits. While many Western people are tending to skip grains (seen as carbohydrates downgraded as fat bombs in some modern diets), TCM views this as a mistake—grains are the primary way to fortify Spleen Qi, particularly whole grain.

The world of food is also governed by the Force of Five. Almost every food is related to other foods and bodily functions through the crosslinking power within its matrix. Here are some specific examples:

FORCE OF FIVE	FIVE ORGANS	FIVE FLAVORS	GRAINS	VEGETABLES	FRUITS AND NUTS
Wood	Liver	Sour	Wheat	Chinese Leek	Plum
Fire	Heart	Bitter	Sorghum	Chinese scallion	Apricot
Earth	Spleen	Sweet	Millet	Soybean seedlings	Date
Metal	Lung	Spicy	Rice	Spring onion	Peach
Water	Kidney	Salty	Beans	Chinese mallow	Chestnut

Eat All Five Flavors: Find balance by eating all of the main five flavors—sour, bitter, sweet, salty, and spicy. Although some people don't like bitter, for example, it's essential to counteract the pathology Fire in the body. For manifestations of Fire—red eyes, pimples, and others—bitter foods can help put out the flame.

Properties of Thermal/Energy: Hot, warm, neutral, cool, cold. Conditions associated with Heat are treated with cool foods, and vice versa. A typical food for a cold (specifically the Wind-Cold type of cold), for instance, is ginger, thanks to its warming properties. It's important in TCM to practice this principle daily, i.e. warm-cool, hot-cold balance.

Some foods for each Energy are shown below:

COLD	COOL	NEUTRAL	WARM	HOT
Watermelon, bitter gourd, kelp, nori, water spinach, honeysuckle, aloe	Millet, mung bean, pear, mango, loquat, lily, tomato, eggplant, tofu, lotus root, wax gourd, chrysanthemum, milk, rabbit	Apple, peach, plum, rice, yellow bean, carrot	Glutinous rice, oats, red dates, Longan arillus, pine nut, garlic, chives, onion, coffee, black tea, chicken	Pepper, cinnamon, mutton, venison

CONGEE CAN BE YOUR MVP

In the U.S., a diverse culture means there's really not one culturally identifiable food. Yet despite similar migratory melting pots, other cultures remain connected to a signature food or foods—pasta and wine in Italy, tortillas and tequila in Mexico, pho in Vietnam, wiener schnitzel in Germany.

In Chinese culture, the need-to-know food is congee—a porridge that's made of grain and most commonly eaten at breakfast. At the top of the home-cooked meal list, just about everyone eats congee just about every day. It's known for its beneficial effects on the body (remember, grain is the foundational food in TCM) to support Spleen Qi, harmonize Stomach Qi, invigorate Spleen deficiency, and strengthen muscles.

The ancients believed congee had three main advantages, it's:

» **Easy to digest**—white rice or yellow millet is gelatinized when its temperature exceeds 60 degrees Celsius/140 degrees Fahrenheit. The water-rich, soft-cooked congee melts in your mouth, making it especially suitable for people with gastrointestinal discomfort.

» **Versatile**—as a base, congee can be combined with a variety of powerful healing ingredients. It's most often eaten as a stand-alone meal with some extras, like meat or fish. See our recipes and suggestions in the Appendix.

» **Full of nutrients**—contains fiber, carbohydrates, and B vitamins to provide strength.

HERBALS HOLD THE POWER

When the Western culture thinks about food, there's usually a lot of talk about the main characters—meat, grains, vegetables, the Grand Teton-sized ice cream sundae. Sure, we talk about the supporting characters—the spices, herbs, and extras that add more flavor—but we don't prop them up with the same importance as our macronutrients and mega-sized dishes.

In Chinese culture, the supporting characters *are* also main characters. That is, herbs and related ingredients provide much of the medicinal fire-power that comes through food. They're not treated as an add-on, but as a must-have. You'll see the most common herbals and related ingredients throughout the rest of *Yin Yang You*. By integrating more of these into your diet and recipes, you'll really maximize the healing power of herbals. TCM's main ones (also used by Western people, of course) include:

INGREDIENT/ FOOD	CONTAINS	EFFECT
Hot tea, black and green	Powerful antioxidants such as gallic acid and catechins	Hot tea is useful to warm the body, improve digestion, and provide mild stimulation via caffeine and theophylline. Drinking freshly brewed tea with cured meats or grilled food can offset some of the effects caused by carcinogens. Tea has the functions of relieving thirst, clearing away Heat, improving eyesight, diuresis, eliminating accumulated fat, sobering up, and prolonging life.
Ginger	Gingerol, which is both an antioxidant and an antimicrobial	In addition to adding flavor to foods, it helps slow spoilage and is a digestive tract stimulant. Ginger has a warming effect that also increases blood flow and helps relieve inflammation. Its functions include relieving nasal obstruction, abdominal pain, cough caused by Coldness, and easing nausea.
Garlic	A sulfur-containing compound called allicin, as well as flavonoids including quercetin, a very powerful antioxidant	It adds pungent, aromatic flavor that enhances the taste of many soups, meats, and vegetable dishes. This cell-signaling compound triggers beneficial effects in the human body. Garlic has the functions of detoxification, detumescence, insecticidal and dysentery, protecting the liver and cardiovascular system, regulating blood sugar levels, and more.
Chili peppers	All fresh capsicum peppers are rich in vitamin C. The spicier varieties contain capsaicin, a fairly powerful natural antimicrobial	The flavor of capsicum peppers can range from very mild, such as common bell peppers to incredibly hot, like Habaneros, Ghost peppers, and Thai chilies. Rich in Vitamin C, it can help tame common colds and flus. Hot peppers are also thought to stimulate blood flow and digestion and the release of endorphins in the brain. Pepper can warm the center and dry Dampness, resist Wind and Cold, improve digestion, open blood flow, and so on.

Ginseng	Chemicals called ginsenosides	The ginseng utilized in Asia is generally much "hotter" than the American Ginseng native to North America. Ginseng has a warming effect and stimulates blood flow, which can be felt immediately after consuming it. Ginseng invigorates Qi, tonifies Spleen and Lung

FOOD FANFARE MATTERS

When we think about healthy eating in the U.S., we tend to focus on the data—calories, fat grams, and so forth. Nutritional choices are made using quantifiable facts about metabolism, calories, and portion size, rather than how they translate to such markers as blood sugar levels, pounds gained, or other hard numbers.

There's been a push in the West to be more mindful of not just what we eat and how much we eat, but also *how* we eat. The idea is the aura around eating has an effect on how foods interact with our bodies. The qualitative data means something, too. What does this look like in practice?

> » **Recognize hunger cues.** Fullness and satisfaction aren't deter-mined by the number of buttons you pop after Thanksgiving dinner. It's subtle—each eater feels hunger cues. Neither too full or too hungry is good. When you feel like you're about 70 percent full, that's the best time to stop. This aligns with the calorie restric-tion health benefits found by Western medicine research. And this 70 percent figure also synchs with Blue Zone research on people (like in Okinawa) who live much longer than the average human.

> » **Keep a regular eating schedule.** Fixed eating times help you sync with your environment and allow your body to work in consistent rhythms (contrary to Western culture that often var-ies eating times or vacillates between periods of gorging and starving). In Traditional Chinese Medicine theory, the circulation of human meridians corresponds with twelve two-hour peri-ods (see previous chapter). For those people who work typical

dawn-to-dusk schedules, the suitable times for eating three meals are between 7:00–9:00 a.m., 11:00 a.m.–1:00 p.m., and 5:00–7:00 p.m. Notice the kitchen closes early in the evening, so you are essentially intermittent fasting for 12 hours.

» **Eat whole foods.** Avoid processed foods filled with ingredients you can't pronounce.

» **Chew your food well and eat slowly.** There's a saying in TCM that "the Spleen opens into the mouth," which implies full digestion of food in the mouth is very beneficial to supporting your Spleen and stomach. Chewing at least 20 to 30 times and swallowing slowly aids digestion.

» **Change where you eat.** Your eating environment should be quiet, tidy, relaxed, and happy. It's not unusual to eat with soft music in the background to help with digestion and absorption.

» **Stay hydrated.** Western medicine often recommends drinking eight glasses of water per day, which is arbitrarily based on old studies. Others argue we should drink until our urine is clear.

LET VARIABLES GUIDE YOU

As you might expect from TCM's use of rhythms and cycles in the universe to influence health, eating is no different. That is, a certain food isn't inherently good or bad, but rather dependent on your place in the universe—as dictated by any number of variables. The most common:

SEASON: Eat warm or hot foods in the cold seasons, and vary your menu during the hotter times of the year. Some guidelines for optimum foods per season include:

» **Spring:** Chinese chives, sweet food like Chinese yam, goji berry, sweet potato

» **Summer:** Watermelon, fresh lotus root, mung bean, cucumber

» **Late Summer:** Poria cocos, coix seed, wax gourd, semen lablab album (what a name!), lotus seed

» **Fall:** dark plum, hawthorn, grape

» **Winter:** warm-natured foods like sticky rice, garlic sprout, pepper, longan, chestnut

TIME: No eating late in the evening. Your metabolism wants to store food at night, leading to a buildup of fat. Three meals a day is essential.

LOCATION: Depending on the climate where you live, you can eat foods that battle pathogens associated with your environment. For instance: In a damp environment, spicy pepper is regarded as a helper for fending off Dampness; whereas for those living in a dry habitat, suitable foods include white wood ear (tremell) and Chinese yam to supplement Yin and offset the loss of bodily fluids.

AGE: Aging in TCM is a process of growing deficiency. The deficiency may manifest at various Organs (Kidney in particular) and in various forms (Qi and Yang in particular). TCM has a set of specialized categories of medicinals (known as tonics) that fight off these deficiencies, and many of them are foods. Chinese yam and Chinese date are among those commonly used.

GENDER: With special physiology, such as menstrual cycle, women are prone to Blood and Qi deficiency. Some foods, such as angelica (DangGui) and goji berry are commonly used in TCM to treat these conditions.

TCM FOOD FLOWCHART

INGESTED FOOD	What you eat and drink
↓	
SPLEEN	Transforms food into essential nutrients, called food essence or Grain Qi
↓	
GRAIN QI	Grain Qi (along with natural air Qi from the lungs and inborn Qi (your genetics) gives rise to Normal Qi
↓	
NORMAL QI	Includes Protective Qi (immunity) and Nutritive Qi (metabolism)

A Note About Supplements

Both Eastern and Western practitioners agree that nutritious food influences longevity: Generally, fresh foods abundant in vegetables, whole grains, nuts, legumes, and lean meat trump a diet containing highly processed foods. But convincing eight billion people to do this day in and day out is about as easy as figuring out how to open a shrink-wrapped package.

Because of this, the world is going to increasingly rely on fortified foods and dietary supplements. In the West, dietary supplements fortified with essential vitamins, minerals, and antioxidants are commonplace, as they fill nutritional gaps in a convenient and cost-effective way. Nutritional supplementation, particularly with vitamins, minerals, and naturally-occurring antioxidants are becoming more common in China every year. This is largely due to Chinese people strongly believing that diseases start from deficiency and their tendency to regard supplements in the same way as tonifying medicinals. In fact, tonifying medicinals are often called supplements, too. For instance, Ginseng is often called a Qi supplement, and date or Longyan a Blood supplement.

In some instances, TCM is readily compatible with dietary supplementation. While purified vitamins and minerals wouldn't appear in any ancient TCM codex—these substances were identified over the past two centuries—nutritional supplementation with vitamins, minerals, and natural antioxidants represents an opportunity to improve global health for millions in a very safe and economical way.

As a matter of fact, researchers have started to study the properties of Western supplements in TCM. Thinking back to our book's Introduction, studies of this sort stem from a fundamental question: Could TCM break its thousand-year-old tradition and adopt a medicinal molecular compound as it does a herb? Successful research in this direction could mean a big leap for integrative medicine.

Black Tea Vs. Green Tea

At your favorite tea shop, there are as many tea flavors as there are colors of crayons. (Pop quiz: Razzle dazzle rose. Is it a tea flavor or a Crayola color?) But the back-to-basics question is this: Which tea—green or black—is healthier? The answer, both—but they do have distinct differences:

» **Green tea**. This non-fermented tea is considered Cold in TCM, since its prepared with rapid-fire baking and maintains the original functional nutrients of tea. According to TCM, green tea is suitable for summer to help clear away Heat, detoxify, and quench thirst.

» **Black tea**. Refined through the typical process of withering, rolling, fermentation, and drying, black tea is a fully fermented tea that is Warm in nature. Therefore, people with Yang deficiency (catch colds often or easily feel cold) are encouraged to drink black tea. Black tea is suitable for winter.

Don't feel like choosing? Consider teas with mild (neutral) properties, such as Wuyi rock tea, which combines green tea and black tea in taste and efficacy.

(Five points if you correctly guessed that razzle dazzle rose is a Crayola color.)

Millet: Another MVP

Because millet does not need refining, it preserves a lot of vitamins (especially B1 and B12) and inorganic salts. TCM believes that millet is the grain of the digestive tract and the most nutritious of the five grains. It is considered sweet and Warm in TCM and, when cooked in porridge, a layer of delicate and nourishing viscous substance (commonly known as "millet oil") floats on it, which is also called "porridge oil."

PART 3

MAJOR PROBLEMS TCM CAN ADDRESS

CHAPTER 7

LOVING EVERY MINUTE*

(well, maybe not that often)

☯

THE THREAT: *Low Libido*
THE TCM SYMBOLIC ORGAN: *Kidney*
THE MISSION OF THE EAST-WEST ALLIANCE: *Supercharge Your Sexual Desire*

W e can all agree that one of the greatest joys in life is being able to share the ups, the downs, the special moments, and even the messes with someone we love. These partnerships, well, they're not easy to explain.

Yes, songwriters, poets, and stars of *The Bachelorette* all have had varying degrees of success describing love. But we *know* it when we *feel* it in all of its emotional depth. Connection, camaraderie, trust, honesty, a mutual understanding that you're really going to lose it if Sweetie Pie dribbles on the toilet seat for what must be the 327th day in a row.

You also know love, lust, passion, and pleasure when you feel it *physically*, as sex serves as an important piece of romantic relationships.

Of course, bedroom tastes and preferences are like tattoos—everybody's is a little bit different. Sex, we know, can be about deep emotional connection or about the immediate physical kind. Or both. So there's no way to say that every person must tango the same way with the same frequency with the same Barry White song in the background. But we can say that—from a health perspective—sex *does* matter.

As we age—and maybe as our relationships change—our sexual desire can fluctuate too. This can happen for hormonal reasons or health-related ones. It can also be caused by stress or other pressures (in the relationship or outside).

On the surface, you may question why there's even a need to address low libido. It's not really a health issue, right? What does it matter to your overall health if you're: a) not having sex as much as you like; or b) don't even have the let's-do-it desire to have sex much at all?

It does matter—for several big reasons.

» Simply, sex feels good. The release of feel-good and connection-with-each-other hormones that happens during and after healthy sex plays a role in mood, which influences stress and health.

» Sex is tied to life span, in that research shows higher-quality sex is associated with better health outcomes and increased longevity.

» Libido isn't just about your desire for romance, release, relaxation, or a risqué romp. It's a proxy for something much bigger: vitality. And vitality really is the centerpiece of the wellness dinner table. When you feel energized, when you live with exuberance, when you're free-flowing with your mojo—that's what gives you the strength and spirit to live stronger, younger, and healthier.

» Libido also plays a role in infertility.

It really is one of the greatest lessons of TCM. We don't always have to be looking to fight off disease or cure a problem. We can use TCM as a vitality booster and a way to think about our bodies as vehicles for living life with joy and youthfulness.

So as we explore ways to increase libido, think of it not only as a form of relationship recess. Instead, think of it as a body-optimizing way to live life in more fulfilling—and fun—ways.

POWER UP YOUR PASSION:
The Biology of Sexual Desire

What revs you up? For some, it can be visual stimulation. For others, it can be emotional stimulation. For hormonally charged teens, it can be any 👏 darn 👏 thing 👏 .

In your younger years, maybe it didn't take too long to go from 0–60. But nowadays? It's not that simple. You don't always just turn the ignition, start the car, and take a ride on the human highway. Libido is much more complex—especially as we get older (though low libido isn't confined to people of a certain age, of course). In Western medicine, we treat low libido as multi-faceted, as it can be a collision of competing factors. When we talk about mind-body connections, there can be no greater example than that of libido—what happens in your mind affects how your body works, or doesn't. Some of the factors that can contribute to low libido include:

» **Hormone decreases and fluctuations:** Most prominently, testosterone, progesterone, and estrogen influence sexual desire. These hormones affect your brain and the "desire" part, but they also influence "function" as well—estrogen may play a role in female lubrication and testosterone can influence erectile function. As we age, these levels drop, prompting therapies that involve increasing hormone levels.

» **Circulatory and other issues:** One of the primary reasons why sexual parts may not work as well as they used to is because of blood flow, responsible for erections and other biological functions important for pleasure for both men and women. Issues involving high blood pressure or heart problems can lead to sexual dysfunction. And when the body parts don't work well, it cycles back to decreased desire. Other health problems also play a role—not just in terms of overtly affecting desire and hormones, but also indirectly. If you suffer from chronic migraines or lower back pain or bloating, the last thing you're thinking about is going to the bedroom for an "important parent meeting."

» **Sexual dysfunction:** If you experience vaginal pain or dryness, erectile issues, ejaculation problems, or other disorders related to the biological mechanics of sex, it affects your sexual desire as well. And it creates a common medical vicious cycle—if you have dysfunction, you have less desire; if you have less desire, you have dysfunction, and so on.

» **Mood:** Any mood issue—stress, depression, anxiety—interferes with libido for the obvious reason. How can you be in the mood to Netflix and chill when you can't even chill in the first place? But it also affects libido in that mood issues interfere with biological pathways that influence sexual desire. So while it may seem obvious you won't be in the mood for fun if you're worried about a job, task, or have financial burden, your body reacts to this stress by altering your ability to feel desire.

» **Psychological barriers:** Here's where the mind-body connection comes most into play as an obvious cause-and-effect of low libido. If you're having relationship trouble, your emotional centers in the brain don't feel the desire to connect the physical centers of your body. And this is why other forms of healing are so important. Your estrogen levels don't mean a thing if your relationship isn't in a great place, underscoring the importance of working on substantive issues that aren't as much about libido as they are about your connection.

So as you look for the fix for low libido, you can see that while there may be pills and tricks for sexual performance, sexual desire is a different story. With multiple possible causes, it's not always easy to pinpoint how and why libido—and vitality—is dwindling. The good news is there are a wide variety of possible treatments and approaches.

THE WESTERN APPROACH TO LOW LIBIDO

MEDICAL: Hormonal therapy, including estrogen, progesterone and testosterone, helps with symptoms associated with loss of sex drive—think vaginal dryness. Some drugs like Addyi and Vyleesi work on the neurotransmitters in the brain to improve libido and are often prescribed in premenopausal women.

LIFESTYLE: Healthy behaviors such as exercise for stress management are often used as front-line defenses for total-body improvement—linked to improved weight, body image, and sex drive.

RELATIONSHIP: The most important body part for sex? The ears. That's because listening is often the missing piece for many couples struggling with lower-quality sex lives. Communication not only means talking about sexual desires, but also opening up about everything. When avenues for understanding get better, so does the road that leads to the bedroom.

THE TCM APPROACH

The TCM version of sexual activity—the umbrella of libido—bears a resemblance to Western medicine. A genetic element called "Congenital Essence" or "Congenital Jing" is inherited from our parents, and "Acquired Essence" or "Acquired Jing" gives functional and nutritional support to the reproductive process. Both Congenital and Acquired Jing (known collectively as Kidney Jing) reside in the Kidney.

TCM attributes low libido to insufficient Kidney Essence or Kidney deficiency. Clinically, Kidney deficiency often appears as a syndrome along with other symptoms such as waist and knee soreness, drab hair, and fatigue. This syndrome is further divided into Kidney Yang deficiency and Kidney Yin deficiency.

Kidney Yang plays a direct role in sexual function and other aspects of health such as bone health, hair growth, memory, and vitality. People with Kidney Yang deficiency show characteristic symptoms of aversion to coldness, preferring hot food and drink, and a voluminous tongue with white fur coat. Kidney Yin is the material support of Kidney Yang. Those with Kidney Yin deficiency show symptoms of dry mouth, bright red tongue that lacks fur coat, hair loss, sunken cheeks, insomnia, and anxiety.

Because of the intricate connection of Kidney, sexual function is associated with other Organs. Acquired Jing comes partly from Food Essence converted by Spleen. Food Essence is transported through Blood coming from the Blood reservoir, Liver. And of course Heart is the Organ that pumps the Blood. Deficiencies in any of these Organs could result in low libido.

For some people with Kidney deficiency, their problem is further complicated by the pathogen Wind, Cold, and Dampness. It's particularly likely for women around menstruation and after labor, as it's believed the increased blood flow makes the Kidney more susceptible to these pathogens. A priority is placed on removing the pathogens before focusing on Kidney reinforcement.

As a libido sidenote, in TCM sex also follows the golden rule: balance. Suppressing your libido is not healthy to maintain a strong, active sex dive, but sexual overindulgence is harmful as well, as depleting Congenital Jing and Kidney Qi compromises your health.

TCM FOR Y-O-U

For better sexual function, it's important to preserve Congenital Jing, supply Acquired Jing with nutritional herbs, and maintain Liver and Kidney health by avoiding harmful habits such as smoking, excessive drinking and sweet-flavored foods, and overwork.

FOOD THERAPY FOR A FIERY LIBIDO

FROM YOUR BELLY...	TO YOUR BODY
Goji berries	Enriches both Blood and Yin energy and tonifies Liver and Kidneys to improve sexual performance
Nuts and seeds (walnuts, almonds, black sesame)	Nourishes Heart and Kidney Essence and enhances sexual performance
Siberian ginseng	Enhances both Yin and Yang energies and promotes blood flow to the significant libido-lifting Organs
Lotus seeds	Strengthens Spleen and Heart and expels Dampness—ideal for low libido caused by deficient Spleen and Heart
Lychee	Complements Kidney Essence and tonifies Blood

A PRACTICE FOR PLEASURE

The ancient Chinese regarded the levator anus exercise as a "sexual enhancement technique." The three meridian vessels—Du Mai, Ren Mai, and Chong Mai—all converge at the Huiyin (perineum) point near the anus. This exercise stimulates these vessels, thereby ensuring sufficient Kidney Qi and Kidney Jing to elevate libido. Complete the levator anus exercise by following these steps:

1. Stand naturally with your legs shoulder-width apart (can also be done while sitting) and both hands close to the outside of your thighs

2. Look straight ahead and relax your arms

3. Inhale through your nose slowly and evenly

4. Concentrate on contracting your abdominal muscles

5. Exhale slowly through your mouth, and at the same time, lift the anus upwards

6. Close the anus tightly and forcefully contract your lower abdomen

7. Hold your breath while keeping the anus lifted for 3–5 seconds

8. Relax your abdomen and anus slowly and then relax your whole body

9. Repeat the above steps for 5–10 minutes, ideally twice daily

MASSAGE/TUINA AND ACUPUNCTURE

Massage (TuiNa) and acupuncture at Changqiang point (the midpoint between the coccyx and anus) may improve sexual function and relieve fatigue after sex. Other acupuncture points, such as the Taichong point (see below), can soothe the Liver, regulate Qi, and improve the function of Kidney Qi.

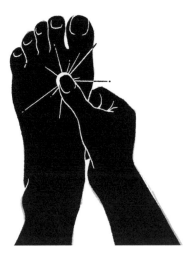

CHAPTER 8

EVERY DOZE HAS ITS THORNS

THE THREAT: *Sleeping Troubles*
THE TCM SYMBOLIC ORGAN: *Heart*
THE MISSION OF THE EAST-WEST ALLIANCE: *Improve Sleep Quality for More Energy and Better Health*

Few health issues inspire more jealousy than ones involving sleep. All around you, everyone seems to be snoozing just fine.

Perhaps you watch your partner dozing for a solid eight hours each night, while you wiggle and squiggle like a fish out of water. Maybe you have a friend who swears melatonin is the answer, while you've tried everything from meds to supplements to warm milk. You may even secretly throw shade to your pup who appears perfectly content as she gallops through a dream-induced field littered with peanut-butter-flavored biscuits.

Sleep troubles are one of our most pervasive health problems, partly because so many things can cause middle-of-the-night disruption—what you've ate or drank, stress level, medical problems, hormone fluctuations, lifestyle factors, nighttime habits, your environment, a neighbor who blasts *Uptown Funk* at 3 a.m.

Insomnia—whether it's not being able to fall asleep or stay asleep—can have dozens of causes, but we all know how it looks and feels.

You're stressed, you're tired, and you need your rest. But every time you try to go to bed, you get distracted by work problems or you need to watch just one more episode of *Parks and Rec*—or you make the fatal mistake of peeking at social media for "just a minute or two" and next thing you know it's 90 minutes later and the only thing you've accomplished is commenting on every single one of @derekhough's dances.

Then you turn out the lights and try to get in those all-important hours before the alarm goes off. But now your mind is racing as you do the equivalent of a gold medal gymnastics routine trying to find a comfortable position. Finally, you fall asleep. Oh great, now you gotta pee! You squeeze in five, maybe six, hours before your alarm startles you from a weird dream involving your dentist, Betty White, and a gas tanker filled with cappuccino. Five snooze buttons later, that tanker of cappuccino sounds delightful—and not an exaggeration. Then, you repeat the cycle again and again, night after restless night.

Sleep serves as one of our fundamental physiological needs. When it's not working well, it can lead to serious consequences. Sleep is when our bodies' systems grow, repair themselves, and do so many other things that fortify our health. So when sleep is inconsistent and dysfunctional in both quantity and quality, we set ourselves up for a whole slew of health issues. For example, lack of shut-eye can be associated with weight gain, heart problems, and cognitive issues—not to mention mood, energy, and overall well-being.

The trick is sleep problems aren't like most medical issues. For many of us, you can't just prescribe a medication, perform surgery, or use some other kind of band-aid treatment. You don't just snap your fingers and— *aha!*—go from a tosser-and-turner to a sweet-dreamer.

This of course makes the case that if you've experienced sleep problems, it's worth exploring TCM treatments and approaches. Looking holistically at how your body interacts with the cycles of the earth and day may help.

SHUT-EYE SHOWDOWN:
THE BIOLOGY OF SLEEP

You already know the basics: Every human needs sleep. Generally, each of us needs between 7 and 9 solid hours for every 24-hour cycle. Sleep patterns are established by our own actions and lifestyle, yes, but they're ultimately governed by circadian rhythms—light and darkness cues and your body's general rhythm throughout the day. For example, a gland deep inside the brain (the pineal gland) gets signals from sunlight to calculate circadian rhythm—the right time to sleep and be awake. These processes are regulated through a variety of chemicals, such as:

ADENOSINE: This compound rises before bedtime. As it gets higher, your body senses it has to fulfill the biological need for sleep, especially if you've been awake for a significant period of time. Caffeine blocks adenosine, which is how it can disrupt sleep patterns.

MELATONIN: This hormone increases in the evening to help your body prepare for sleep. The light-dark cycle of the day plays a role in how your body makes and releases melatonin. When you expose yourself to bright and artificial lights at night, it disrupts the release and upsets your sleep.

Now, all sleep is not created equal. Your body moves through different stages of sleep several times throughout the night. With four stages of non-REM sleep—ranging from light/wakefulness to deep sleep and then REM (rapid eye movement) when your brain activity is high—you'll cycle through this whole 80 to 90 minute sequence multiple times per night.

During this time, granted, you're not doing anything. You're asleep after all. So what's the big deal if you don't quite get enough sleep? But that's not the way to think about it.

Here's how: When you have a package that needs to ship to the other side of the country overnight, you pay FedEx or UPS to get it there. You drop it in the bin, and it shows up at an office 3,000 miles away the next morning. A whole system of workers—drivers to pilots to sorters to deliverers—help the package arrive. It happens quickly, efficiently, and behind-the-scenes. What's that have to do with sleep?

Your body is essentially one big FedEx facility. While you're asleep, your whole body is working hard. It's repairing cells that were damaged during the day. The cells wash themselves of any daily toxins accumulated—and not just from bad thoughts. It's growing new neurons and neural connections. It's getting stronger. In fact, one part of your immune system functions better when you're asleep (it's why people who sleep less are more vulnerable to getting sick). Sleep is basically the time when you're cleaning up the whole chemical and cellular mess that happens when you live, eat, and move.

It's working while you're not.

So when you don't get enough sleep—or enough quality sleep—your biological workers are on an extended lunch break. They don't do anything. And what does this mean for you? You've got it. Without quality shut-eye your cellular repairs don't happen, putting you at risk for chronic disease, weight gain, or developing any number of health problems.

You likely already know about good sleep hygiene—the tranquil routines that can help you sleep, like limiting screen time before bed, cutting back on caffeine starting in the afternoon, and keeping your bedroom calm and dark. These nighttime rituals don't just establish healthy habits, they're recommended to help maximize your biology. With good sleep hygiene, you're trying to get your body's natural systems, compounds, and sleep/wake cycles working in your favor.

THE WESTERN APPROACH TO SLEEP ISSUES

SLEEP HYGIENE: Practice good habits—a cool and dark room, shutting down all screens at least an hour before bed, etc.—to help induce sleep. Also try waking up at the same time each morning to get into a regular rhythm. And avoid alcohol and stimulants like caffeine, which can disrupt your chemical, sleep-inducing processes.

MEDICINAL TREATMENTS: GABA—an inhibitory neurotransmitter—is formed by neurons in the sleep center of the brain. Pharmacologists have invented small molecules that bind to and activate GABA receptors, thereby mimicking GABA activity to help you sleep. These kinds of drugs, like Ambien and Valium, do have side effects similar to "hangover" symptoms (drowsiness, headache, weakness, dizziness). And for some people, dependence and tolerance are problems.

SUPPLEMENTS: A melatonin supplement safely supports your body's natural process of releasing melatonin in evening hours. It's the most popular non-pharmacological sleep aid.

OTHER APPROACHES: Exercise is touted as a sleep aid, in that regular activity is associated with better sleep (though it may disrupt sleep if done too closely to bedtime).

THE TCM APPROACH

As you would expect with Yin-Yang Theory, night is Yin (restive) and day is Yang (active). And sleep is vital for Yin-Yang balance. Insomnia swings the Yin-Yang balance bringing the body into various states of deficiencies, and from there all kinds of problems follow.

In Chapter 5 under TCM Chronotherapy, we listed a clockwise to-do list for the 12 meridians. From 9 p.m. to 5 a.m., all tasks are sleep related. This is the TCM version of the circadian clock.

Now, how is sleep controlled in TCM biology? In TCM, insomnia is a disorder of the Spirit (a term to describe the entire mental state), which is why it's often associated with Heart (which governs Spirit) deficiency and loss of Heart function on the Yin-Yang balance. Treatment works to restore both balance and Spirit.

Insomnia often falls under four syndromes:

Heart–Spleen deficiency: Beyond insomnia, symptoms also include palpitation, chest pain or tightness, poor memory, poor appetite, sluggish bowel movement, low energy, etc.

Heart Yin deficiency with asthenic Fire: Palpitation or irregular heartbeat, poor memory, dry mouth, and feeling hot in palms and soles.

Heart–Gallbladder deficiency: Heart palpitation, dreaminess, easily scared, very light sleep.

Heart–Kidney disharmony: Palpitation, dizziness, memory loss, lower back pain, etc.

While we tend to think of insomnia as an isolated sleeping problem, TCM sees it as part of a bigger picture. Oftentimes, insomnia (insomnia here being a clue to something bigger happening in the body) goes hand in hand with depression and anxiety. Both have similar neurologic disturbances, which is why sedative/hypnotic drugs often improve both conditions. Interestingly, in TCM, both fall under the pathology of Heart Fire (see Heart Yin deficiency above).

Given wakefulness is controlled by multiple neurotransmitters, it could play a role in the Yin and Yang balance of Spirit. The neuronal pathways controlling wake or sleep are complicated, but by and large, they are divided into two categories: stimulant (like dopamine) and inhibitory (like adenosine and gamma-amino-byturic acid (GABA). Caffeine keeps you awake by turning off the adenosine pathway, and sleeping pills like Ambien and Valium work by turning on the GABA pathways. Insomnia is largely attributed to the imbalance of these neurotransmitters. Of course, it remains to be seen if TCM insomnia therapies change the levels of these signaling compounds, but it would be an exciting research area of integrative medicine.

TCM FOR Y-O-U

With many possible options to help you address sleep (including improving your sleep hygiene), you can also use TCM therapies to help move into a regular pattern.

Soak Your Feet: Results can improve with continued use.

1. Add 3 large pieces of ginger to a pot of water large enough fit both feet
2. Bring to a boil
3. Take off heat and add 1 Tbsp. vinegar
4. Let cool until the water will not scald your feet
5. Soak your feet for 30 minutes (continuously adding hot water to maintain temperature)

FOOD THERAPY FOR BETTER BEDTIMES

FROM YOUR BELLY...	TO YOUR BODY
Wild jujube porridge	Address a Heart-Spleen deficiency by cooking a rounded ½ cup of Japonica rice and adding 1 Tbsp. of wild jujube
Lotus seed congee	Provides a calming effect and helps address Heart-Kidney disharmony. Boil, then simmer blanched lotus seeds for 30 minutes, add to glutinous rice, and simmer until thick
Luffa nectar drink	To fight Heart-Yin deficiency, peel 1 Tbsp. of luffa, mince, then grind. Mix with 2 ½ tsp. honey
Licorice-wheat-date soup	Mix licorice (1 ¾ tsp.), whole wheat (1 ¾ tsp.), date (10 pieces), add to 4 cups water, and boil and simmer for 30 min. Helps with Heart-gallbladder deficiency

SELF-MASSAGE YOURSELF TO SLEEP

WHERE	ACU POINT	TCM THEORY	WHAT TO DO	LOCATE IT
The depression between the outer sinews on the wrist line when flexing the fingers	"Shenmen"	The gateway for Spirit to get in and out so it can help calm the mind and help you sleep	Press the point before going to bed	
The depression of the occipital bone behind the ear	"Fengchi"	Calms the mind to help those with Heart Yin deficiency with asthenic Fire	Place both thumbs on the two sides of the point and then press/ rub the point for 1 minute. Repeat 5 times	
One finger width next to the tibia and four fingers' width below the connection of the two eyes (protrusions) of the outer knee	"Zusanli"	Helps those with Heart-Spleen deficiency	Tap and knead on the point for 5 minutes on each side until it becomes warm	
Hair	N/A	Promotes circulation of Qi and Blood to calm the mind and promote sleep	Comb your hair with your fingers for 5 to 10 minutes at a time	
3 fingers' width above the inner ankle bone	"Sanyinjiao"	Helps insomnia in general	Press and knead on the point for 5 minutes on each side until it becomes warm	

CHAPTER 9

G.I. WOE

THE THREAT: *Digestive Disturbance*
THE TCM SYMBOLIC ORGAN: *Spleen*
THE MISSION OF THE EAST-WEST ALLIANCE: *Calm a Turbulent Digestive System*

In your life, your midsection has endured its fair share of tumult. You might remember a literal punch to the gut or a tortuous plank workout, or you might flashback to a bad bout of food poisoning, a knockout flu, or an ill-advised rendezvous with tequila.

No matter what threats your belly has fought off, make no mistake—your gut has guts.

Strong, resilient, and able to tolerate #NaughtyNastyNachos in a single bound, your digestive system does indeed have superhero abilities when it comes to processing, filtering, and dispatching ("bile, please report to quadrant four for nacho cleanup duty").

All of its strength, though, doesn't mean it's a foolproof system. Its rich ecosystem and biological intricacies introduce vulnerabilities. Some of these hiccups are indeed self-inflicted (what we eat can disrupt ideal operations), while some are much more nuanced and complex.

Call these digestive disruptions what you want—belly aches, tummy troubles, GI issues, volcanic explosions of a bathroom-destroying magnitude. In any case, they generally fall into the same umbrella category: Something doesn't feel quite right, and that uneasiness manifests itself in such symptoms as diarrhea, constipation, bloating, general stomach upset, and a feeling a bit "off."

It's not surprising that GI troubles influence your mood and overall well-being. The reason why the GI system is often called the "second brain" is because it's filled with hormones and chemicals your brain needs. The feel-good hormone serotonin circulates there, for example. So when something's off with your belly, your mood can sense it too.

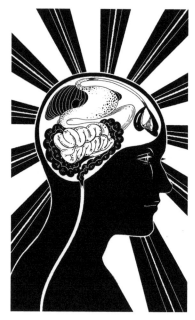

And that's why GI issues are so important. While it may seem they can be quickly solved with an over-the-counter medication or waiting out the distress, the truth is GI trouble really does work in biological cycles.

Some days you can have calm waters. On other days those corn-polluted waves can be strong, choppy, stormy, and terrifying. They come and go. But sometimes it overwhelms you, destroying everything in its path. And that's why a more holistic approach to making your waters calmer over the long haul makes sense.

By really experimenting with different approaches and remedies, you can begin to fine-tune your body and how all of the systems work.

After all, GI problems have been around as long as mankind has existed, yet they're still so common it feels right to go with our gut and bring every healing technique we know into the proverbial ring. As is the case with many chronic issues, two heads are better than one—that is,

TCM isn't treating a commonly understood problem in a different way, but rather coaching us differently, giving some complementary solutions in a Western medicine-dominated society.

Picture yourself having some control over the strength and volume of those waves. But it's not an on-off switch. It's more like a dial you're finely tuning just right. A little here, a wee bit there and… "Thank god it's the first time I've pooped in four days!"

When you do this (fine-tune, not poop), you have a better chance of finding what works to settle your stomach, spending more time living with a better belly.

MIDDLE MANAGEMENT:
The Biology of Your Gut

Your digestive system is a lot like other parts of your body. You don't give it a second thought until something goes wrong. Right? No need to think about the automatic process of digestion when it's all running smoothly. You eat a bit, you expel a bit, and you go on with your life, doing it again and again (the average person produces about 300 pounds of poop per year).

To understand what might be going wrong with general upset—often called irritable bowel syndrome (IBS) as a catch-all disorder for all kinds of GI distress—it does help to think a bit about what's happening inside your gastrointestinal environment. IBS affects nearly a quarter of Americans—with the severity ranging from inconvenience (when you gotta go…) to extreme pain and discomfort. Let's look at the two main inner workings of your gut:

THE DIGESTIVE SYSTEM: This system encompasses every part of the digestive highway from your mouth to your anus. But what happens between those points is less of an interstate and more a system of roads and side streets that are home to how your food gets processed into nutrients and waste.

A brief overview: As food moves from your mouth to your esophagus, your control of the digestive process ends (choosing and chewing your food) and your system takes over as pilot. The act of swallowing signals your brain to start the process of peristalsis—the action and movement to shuttle food along the highway. At this point, a variety of hormones and nerves influence everything from hunger to cravings to the speed of the digestive process.

As food enters your stomach, digestive juices from your pancreas, liver, and other organs mix with it before moving through to your small intestine. This where water gets absorbed and digested nutrients move to your bloodstream—sent off to take energy through the roads and side streets—to various organs, tissues, and systems of your body. Waste from this process moves to the large intestine, where water is once again absorbed and stool is formed to prepare for bodily elimination.

It's easy to see how—with all the movement and influencing factors—the dynamics of digestion can get upset. Hormone levels, nerve signaling, interaction with various foods can all influence not only the process, but how your body reacts and how you feel. Disruption manifests itself as general upset or the more extreme constipation and diarrhea.

From a medical standpoint, our goal is to settle the process to avoid the storms. Because of the complexity and individual nuances of every person's systems, there's no one fix for chronic problems (acute gut-related issues can often be relieved or alleviated with various medications). This is why TCM therapies and approaches may be especially helpful for people who suffer from chronic symptoms related to IBS.

THE MICROBIOME: For a long time, we tended to think about our gut mainly in the way it's described above—as a process that involves various organs and movements to break down food and either use it for energy, store it as fat, or expel it from the body.

In recent years, there's been a greater emphasis on the microbiome—the ecosystem of trillions of bacteria, fungi, viruses, and other organisms that live within our body. Impressively, we have 10 times more bacteria in our gut than cells in our body. Made of tens of thousands of bacterial species, everyone's microbiome is different. One important measure of the healthiness of the microbiome—as with any complex ecosystem—is its diversity. The main point here is we really outsource our digestion. Healthy foods maintain a balanced, diversity-rich microbiome, whereas junk foods lead to disproportionate growth of some bacteria and decreased diverseness.

But here's the thing: You can't really assess if the microbiome as working or not in the same way you would, say, analyze how much an artery is blocked. It's more like an middle-school orchestra. Sometimes, it plays the tune well, sometimes a few notes are off, and sometimes you can't tell what the heck they're trying to play. But with your microbiome, there's more at stake than just a rendition of *We Will Rock You*.

Making it even tougher is your microbiome is constant flux—changing daily and over long periods of time. Affected by nutrition and other factors, the microbiome can help protect against disease and aid digestion. While there's still a lot of research that needs to be done to evaluate the role of the microbiome, it's worth noting there are ways to help balance the bacteria in your gut to help promote better health and overall digestive well-being.

THE WESTERN APPROACH TO DIGESTIVE ISSUES

OVER-THE-COUNTER MEDS: A variety of medications can relieve symptoms, such as Imodium® and Pepto Bismol® for diarrhea. Laxatives can assist with constipation, as can stool softeners or mineral oil, which help lubricate the bowel to promote movements. Fiber supplements also aid in the digestive process.

NUTRITION: Popular nutritional choices to help with digestive issues include increasing both water intake (helps move the stool) and fiber (can improve digestive movement). Yogurt and kefir help enhance the flora in your gut to improve the balance of your microbiome.

> **PREBIOTIC AND PROBIOTIC SUPPLEMENTS:** Help to replenish and fortify the good bacteria in your gut by providing them with good nutrition.
>
> **COLOSTRUM:** Increasingly more popular, with Western research supporting its role in calming the gut. This makes sense, since the first milk from a mother is essential to helping a new born infant's intestines grow and prosper in its new environment. The dozens of important proteins in colostrum help intestinal recovery and support a healthy microbiome.

THE TCM APPROACH

In TCM, digestion is broken down a little differently. The food you eat is processed into either helpful parts or waste. The useful parts ("food Essence") can be channeled through the Spleen (the transformer and transporter), where they're used to help fortify Blood, fluids, Qi, and provide all the nutrients the body needs. Recall TCM Organs are functional instead of anatomical. Like the virtual presence of an internet "cloud" run by servers from multiple locations, Spleen is the superimposition of all parts that contribute to digestion—including intestine, stomach, liver, pancreas, and the gallbladder.

Any GI problems—like indigestion, nausea, abdominal pain, loose bowels, and constipation—could come from Spleen deficiency. As usual, the loss of Yin-Yang balance happens as the root cause. What follows is the invasion of pathogens (evils). For instance, Spleen invaded by Dampness typically results in diarrhea; constipation occurs if there's concurrent Heat in stomach and Intestine; and abdominal pain could be the result of accompanying Liver Qi stagnation. This explains the diverse symptoms of common GI illnesses such as IBS.

So here are some major syndromes with GI problems:

Spleen deficiency–Loose stool, pale and plump tongue, sallow complexion, vague abdominal pain, no appetite heaviness of limbs.
Cold-dampness fettering the Spleen–No appetite, clear urine, slow pulse, abdominal pain, heaviness of limbs.
Heat assembling in the Intestines and Stomach–Dry stool, distention and fullness of the abdomen and even pain, red tongue and yellow dry coating, dry mouth, bad breath, vexation.
Stagnation of Liver and Spleen Qi–Distention, abdominal pain, dry stool, irritable or sullen.

Interesting to note about Liver Qi stagnation, people who have digestive issues also tend to have some kind of emotional and sleep disruptions too. The West also sees the link, but more often through hormones and neurotransmitters in the gut and brain. TCM sees the connection through a virtual Organ, Liver, that clears the runway of Qi and so prevents many issues.

Spleen deficiency could be a result of excessive consumption of alcohol, coffee, tea, cold raw food, soft drinks, and sweets, as well as overthinking. Foods produced by modern agriculture and industry, especially highly processed foods, lack nourishing Essence and increase the burden for Spleen. Such foods slowly deplete Spleen Qi and cause indigestion. Perhaps this explains partly why nowadays, despite an abundant food supply, digestive problems such as IBS and food allergy have become increasingly common. In addition, Chinese medicine holds that different emotions are related specifically to Organs, and overthinking damages the function of Spleen.

Does TCM also cover cutting-edge microbiome science? The answer is likely yes. As we explained above, the Spleen is an all-in-one functioning Organ that comprises different physical parts. Microbiome fits into one of the parts. Renzhonghuang is used to treat diseases by using the microbial flora in the feces of healthy children. Studies have found TCM medicinals that strengthen Spleen stimulate the growth of beneficial gut flora.

TCM FOR Y-O-U

Look to the remedies below, along with others like acupuncture and cupping, to help ease various GI problems you may be experiencing.

FOOD THERAPY TO QUIET GI TROUBLE

FROM YOUR BELLY...	TO YOUR BODY
Rice or millet porridge	Rice has the effect of tonifying Qi, strengthening Spleen and Stomach, and eliminating thirst—the fine viscous substances floating like ointment on the top of rice porridge is commonly known as "rice oil" and helps relieve diarrhea
Cucumber and Chinese cabbage	Helps with constipation resulting from Heat assembling in the intestines
Bamboo shoots	Aids in relieving constipation from stagnation of Liver and Spleen Qi
Chinese yam	Peel and steam for 30 min. Helps Spleen deficiency
Bergamot congee	Helps with constipation—cook 1 ⅓ Tbsp of bergamot in water, then add ½ cup of cooked japonica rice and a little rock sugar, to taste

SELF-MASSAGE TO SOOTHE YOUR STOMACH

WHERE	ACU POINT	TCM THEORY	WHAT TO DO	LOCATE IT
4 fingers' width above the navel	"Zhongwan"	Smooths the running of the Spleen and Stomach meridian to help with various GI problems	Place one hand on the point and another on top of it to reinforce pressure. Gently press and rub (2 to 3 minutes)	
Three finger widths from both sides of the navel	"Tianshu"	Helps with various GI symptoms	These points should be massaged clockwise for about 10 minutes for constipation, counterclockwise for diarrhea	

Zusanli acupoint massage can also help strengthen the function of the Spleen and Stomach.

GET MOVING

There's an old Chinese saying: "Walk after you dine, live up to 99." It's well-documented in TCM scriptures that an after-dinner, slow-paced walk helps tonify the Spleen. In addition, this movement can help with weight loss, which usually improves digestive issues.

CHAPTER 10

WHAT THE FUNK

☯

THE THREAT: *Depression / Mood Issues*
THE TCM SYMBOLIC ORGAN: *Liver*
THE MISSION OF THE EAST-WEST ALLIANCE: *Improve Your Mood to Feel Better and Be Healthier*

There's no doubt the way you feel fluctuates—from day to day, hour to hour, even from sentence to sentence. Some days it may seem as if you're surfing on a rainbow, and other days you may feel as anxious as the soon-to-be-axed victim in a horror flick.

Mood—good, bad, or somewhere in between—is like that. It can come in waves, change based on almost an infinite amount of variables, and blanket you like a comfy quilt.

In the history of Western medicine, issues like depression, anxiety, and mood disorders have played second fiddle to hard-core medical dilemmas like heart problems and cancer. But we've grown to know matters of mood are every bit as much of a medical issue as any other. The trouble is there are no easy diagnoses and solutions because, well, mood dysfunctions are far less tangible than many other medical conditions. While you can see cancer cells or a clogged artery in a high-tech diagnostic, there's no machine that can scan the brain and tell you feel a wee bit wacked-out today.

And frankly, you don't need a machine to spit out this diagnosis—you know it, you feel it, you live it. The danger of depression is multifaceted—mood and depression issues are problems because of how you feel and function, but they're also a threat due to of the cascading effect they can have on your health.

You feel bad. You search for something to make you feel good. You grab a glass—or seven—of wine, or enough banana bread to feed a football team. The next thing you know, you've slid down the rabbit hole of addiction, weight problems, stress, sleep disruptions, and more.

That's because mood influences action and behavior.

The main hurdle when it comes to treating mood issues is it's a little like pain—you can feel it, but we don't always know the cause. Perhaps that's why TCM approaches make a lot of sense here, taking a holistic look at as many variables and treatment options as possible.

What gets tricky is mood issues really do run the spectrum of severity. Everything from major depression—where the person can be a danger to themselves or others, to everyday mood disorders, when feeling blue affects everyday life, but may not have life-threatening consequences. Western medicine does have a variety of ways to handle both ends of the spectrum—and all forms in between—but if you struggle with mood and anxiety, it's worth considering TCM approaches as part of your toolkit. Fact in point, mood disorders have been around as long as humans have existed. The angst of moodiness is what propels us to work out solutions (when something doesn't feel right, we try to correct it). So if we can learn the gentle tools that have worked for 5,000 years, we will be better armed to tame our demons.

Just know, this isn't about eliminating all anxiety, but harnessing it for good.

While we're pretty sure humans weren't designed to be residents of cloud nine all the time, we do think it's possible to nudge your mood in a more positive direction, which does improve your overall health.

It's also worth noting the pandemic of 2020 certainly put an even stronger spotlight on mental health. As more people grappled with stress, anxiety, depression, fear, and other complex and serious emotions, we all looked for ways to fight through the funk. It wasn't/isn't/won't be easy, and there's no switch to flip to automatically pull you out of tough times, but we believe in the idea of biological reinforcements—allowing nature's medicine to massage your biology to a better place.

MOODY BLUES:
The Biology of Depression

This probably goes without saying, but we will anyway: The brain—as its own 3-pound biological galaxy—is the most complex and least understood organ of the body. The same organ that gives us the ability to think, solve problems, love, laugh, write smashingly nifty song lyrics, build rockets, and dream about your childhood neighbor playing ukulele in a bathtub of orange peels is also the one that can make you feel like all the color drained out of the world.

So in essence, here's what we know in Western medicine about the causes of depression and mood issues: We *don't* know.

Such issues can be triggered by many factors, and they're likely a lot more complex than just the "chemical imbalance" often referred to in these cases. Some possible causes and links include:

SOFTWARE ISSUES: Indeed, brain function relies on thousands of chemical interactions, and when they malfunction, it can contribute to depression and mood issues. However, the fallacy is you can just dial up or dial down certain chemicals to get to the "right" levels. Brain chemistry is so complex that chasing a specific chemical reaction often doesn't lead to a snap-out-of-it cure.

HARDWARE ISSUES: There's some evidence that people who have depression have a smaller hippocampus (memory-storage center of the brain) than those who don't. Depression may also be linked to the inability of neurons (the nerve cells of your brain) to efficiently and effectively talk to each other. This is important because miscommunication between neurotransmitters may lead to faulty messaging linked to chemical reactions tied to depression. If your brain doesn't send or get the right signals, the faulty wiring disrupts normal brain function. One theory is new neurons need to grow in order to improve mood.

GENETICS: Research shows people with a family history of depression have an increased chance of getting it themselves. As many genes do influence mood, it's not surprising there may be a connection here. It's important to note that genetic disposition doesn't necessarily define your health destiny. The field of epigenetics suggests we have the ability to turn genes on and off and change the way they're expressed. Which means, just because you have a certain gene doesn't guarantee it will function the same way it did for others. Our bodies can adjust to the environment (like famine or

stress) by hardwiring a change of our DNA on the fly—changes that can even have an effect on our children when we pass genes to them.

ENVIRONMENTAL FACTORS: In the very broadest of terms—what factors are changing the environment of your brain? Medications or medical conditions can influence it, so can stress and stressful events. We all know traumatic life events change the way we feel. And of course your literal environment can impact your mood (i.e. seasonal affective disorder happens during dark winter months when people are exposed to less sunlight).

With causes so widely varied, it begs the question: When we don't know the root of the issue, how do we effectively treat it? Typically, the West looks to a variety of methods—medications to help regulate mood, or lifestyle or behavior therapies such as exercise or talking to a professional. Many methods have some success, but they're far from universally effective. This is the sweet spot for TCM. When Western medicine lacks a clear diagnosis or treatment, TCM can fill in the gaps.

And when we're talking about a condition with so many variables, it may be worth looking into a treatment approach that helps balance Qi to improve mood or alleviate depression.

THE WESTERN APPROACH TO MOOD ISSUES

PREVENTION: Exercise is shown to help prevent the onset of depression and can have a dramatic effect on recurring depressive symptoms.

MEDICINAL TREATMENTS: Antidepressants mostly act on the neurotransmitters that control mood, such as serotonin, dopamine, and norepinephrine. They work in a variety of ways to help either improve their current function or stop them from degrading. Side effects often occur, and they do not work as well for people with a explainable reason to be depressed, like a recent tragedy. They also tend to lose some effect over time.

TALK THERAPY: Talking to a professional like a therapist, or even to a friend or family member, can have major benefits in working out the issues that bring you down. Our brains grew to their current size in order to see each other's faces and hear others' voices. So use your head to get out of your head.

OTHER APPROACHES: Because there's no one direct cause or treatment, many lifestyle strategies can help. For example, besides prevention, light therapy—being exposed to UV light in winter months—has been shown to raise the spirits. Taking Vitamin D (the Sunshine Vitamin) can also brighten your day. Sunlight releases mood-boosting serotonin, while also triggering Vitamin D synthesis. It's why even a leisurely afternoon stroll can be a good one-two punch to heighten your mood.

THE TCM APPROACH

TCM has its own psychology and psychiatry. Mental activities are named Shen or Spirit in TCM, and they're part of the function of the Heart. To go by the principle of Force of Five, Spirit consists of five components:

1. Mood—distinctive emotional quality or character.
2. Corporeal soul—instinct or the animating part of one's mind.
3. Ethereal soul—the moral and spiritual part of the human being.
4. Consciousness—act or power of thinking and forming ideas.
5. Will—mental power by which a person can direct his thoughts and actions.

TCM recognizes mood as a critical factor in mental and physical health. Recall the five moods under Force of Five in Chapter 5. Remarkably, each mood corresponds to one Organ, and excess emotions lead to Organ-specific injuries, i.e., excess joy does harm to the Heart, anger to Liver, worry to Spleen, sadness to Lung, and fear to Kidney.

On the other hand, the TCM Organs affect the moods. The Liver is the well-known "uplifter." It serves as a "dredger," a highly abstracted function that safeguards the smoothness of any physiological process. It's also interesting that the Chinese term for depression is Yi Yu (meaning suppression or melancholy). It makes sense that Liver Qi stagnation is considered the major cause of depression. Think of it metaphorically. When Mother Nature's force is suppressed, sadness builds up like dewdrops from encumbered vapor.

Liver Qi stagnation is a common TCM pathology. Keep in mind the TCM Organs are functional. The term applies to anywhere the Qi movement is impeded. It manifests as Qi stagnation syndrome and can be seen through the process of syndrome differentiation. Depression is one prominent symptom of this syndrome, yet over time, pent-up Qi brings further Organ damage. TCM has a term for this: "pent-up Qi transforms to Fire."

Fire is the major pathogen for insomnia, constipation, anxiety, etc., which may be due to Qi stagnation.

Liver Qi stagnation is essentially a problem of Liver deficiency. This ties depression to the fundamentals of this book, Yin-Yang balance. Here's another way to look at depression from the Yin-Yang angle. Why does basking in the sun help depression? Recall that Yang is on the more dynamic and energetic side, which is the opposite of stagnation. Sunlight, in Chinese, literally means "the light of Yang." Not surprisingly, in TCM, sunlight is also seen to help rebalance the Yin and Yang, thereby clearing the runway for the movement of Qi.

Life often throws hard balls our way and disrupts the Yin-Yang balance. To maintain equilbrium, we must learn to adapt to change—in much the same way we alter how we dress and the foods we eat for each new season.

TCM FOR Y-O-U

We don't claim there's a quick fix for mood problems, especially if they're severe. But you can nudge yourself into a better direction with some strategies to help address mental health.

FOOD THERAPY TO GET DE-FUNKED

FROM YOUR BELLY...	TO YOUR BODY
Mint tea	Soothes the Liver to help relieve depression, anxiety, and tension
Rose chrysanthemum lavender tea	Mix rose (½ tsp.), Chrysanthemum (½ tsp.), and lavender (½ tsp.) in a cup of boiling water. Drink and refill multiple times
Yujin-lianzi rice porridge	Helps improve mood—combine turmeric (*Curcuma family*) root tuber 1 ¾ Tbsp., lotus seed 1 ½ Tbsp., japonica rice ½ cup and cook with 2 cups of water

SELF-MASSAGE TO PERK UP

WHERE	ACU POINT	TCM THEORY	WHAT TO DO	LOCATE IT
The depression between the outer sinews on the wrist line when flexing the fingers	"Shenmen"	This gateway for Spirit to enter and leave us can help calm the mind and improve mood	Press the point before going to bed	
The top of the and the hollow area underneath the base of the skull on either side	"Baihui" and "Fengchi"	Helps relieve symptoms related to Spirit	Massage "Baihui" until it slightly hot. Press "Fengchi" point" for 1 minute and then press the temple for 1 minute	
About 4 fingers' width above the horizontal line of your wrists and between the two outer tendons	"Neiguan"	Helps relieve symptoms related to the Spirit	Massage for 10–15 minutes	

TAKE A HOT BATH

When you're in a state of tension and anxiety, your body's circulation is low. Hot water can promote blood circulation as well as the flow of Qi. When Blood and Qi run normally, the body relaxes. At the same time, try taking a deep breath—slowly breathing in and out helps to reduce excitability within the nervous system to restore a sense of calm. You can also try mindfulness meditation to focus on your body, breath, and mind. If you cannot take a bath, blow a hot hair dryer on your navel until you feel warm inside, and then take deep breaths for five minutes. This may bring you instant relief from a bad mood.

CHAPTER 11

HOUSE OF GUARDS

☯

THE THREAT: *The Common Cold*
THE TCM SYMBOLIC ORGAN: *Lung*
THE MISSION OF THE EAST-WEST ALLIANCE: *Optimize the Immune System to Protect the Inside from Attacks from the Outside*

A cold is sort of like a biological traffic jam. Sure, it's almost as annoying as a phone battery at 2%, but at least we know relief is just around the corner and the jam will be over soon enough. It's a temporary health annoyance.

Yes, we know the cold isn't the same kind of ailment as the ones we detailed in the previous four chapters. Those conditions are all ones that can be chronic, severely debilitate your life, and contribute to serious health consequences. So it might seem as if we're shoehorning the common cold into the same big-picture category as a digestive system that sounds like a helicopter propellor.

But let's look at what the common cold is really about. It's about learning how the immune system works, how you can fortify and optimize it, the TCM approach for your biological defense system, and ways you can strengthen your forces against all kinds of attacks.

Now, we understand the biggest immune issues on your mind—things like heart disease and COVID—are the real life-threateners and, therefore, the real worries. And as we alluded to in the early part of *Yin Yang You*, there are some health issues—cancers, heart conditions, and more—the West simply addresses really well because of the charge of scientific advances. So we won't be detailing those kinds of diseases in this book.

Take this chapter for what it is—a peek into the immune system to help you squash the unmet medical needs you encounter when it comes to bacterial and viral infections. And look into what you might do to strengthen your immunity, which can be important when you're faced with more serious problems.

After all, we know what it feels like when you get hit with a bad cold. You're as energetic as an ottoman, your head feels like the entire population of Leavenworth is trying to jailbreak through your skull, and your nose is stuffed like a Thanksgiving bird. #WithAWholeLotOfGravy

No, a cold isn't the end of the world. It won't destroy your being or do much to change your life. Though you may be annoyed you have to dump out a dozen trash bins of mucus-crunched tissues. The real issue is it *can* mess up your mojo, whether for mere hours or a few days. And your response is a barometer of your readiness for battle when bigger threats arise.

In the interest of overall health optimization, let's talk about how to strengthen your immune system. Learning how to prevent or treat the common cold can be just one of your many tools for building a stronger, healthier, and more energetic body.

PROTECTION AGAINST INFECTION:
The Biology of the Immune System

The mission of your immune system is to protect your body against anything that tries to threaten it. It's a finely built defensive system—various cells and systems with different jobs and roles attempting to keep things running smoothly.

Your immune system is divided into two categories: Innate immunity are immune responses that kick in right after they're exposed to a threat. Your skin, for example, is a protective barrier built to shun foreign entities that may be harmful. Adaptive immunity is a complex system that operates by identifying and remembering invaders and then creating a slew of cells and molecules (e.g. antibodies) to fight against a very specific threat. Both work to protect you in different ways, though they have the similar mission to keep your body working in its natural, optimized, balanced state.

In this state, your body churns and chugs the way it should. It works like a mini factory, and if everything hums along, you don't feel a thing. You function the way you're supposed to.

So now let's picture this factory produces the most precious of commodities. And it is! You!

You don't just leave the factory with wide-open doors for any evil-doers to walk in and take the goods, set fire to the machinery, or steal the system software. You protect it.

That's what your immune system does.

Your biological factory has a lot of windows and doors. The most common openings are the nose and mouth that interact most often with the outside world and are vulnerable to foreign invaders, like bacteria and viruses.

Invaders may try to enter the factory in a stealthy way, and sometimes they brazenly just knock on the door and ask to enter. In any case, some cells in your immune system have the job of checking their ID. They inspect to see if it's a foreign body or welcome to come in. If it's foreign, they call in the killer cells to handle these invaders. With auto-immune issues, the immune cell guards launch friendly fire on innocent cells belonging to our own bodies—clearly checkpoint confusion, and yet this unfortunate scenario serves as a strong reminder of the importance of Yin-Yang balance.

Assuming the cell guards are in top form, the fight is on. Killer B and T cells come to attack and, well, get busy. They start latching onto the foreign cells to escort them out of the body. It can be an ugly firefight. They both have a serious mission. The foreign cells are looking for a place to live, and the immune cells are telling them to get off their lawn.

This is the point where you *feel* it.

All of these symptoms—the runny nose, the sneezing, the coughs, the headaches—are the immune battles taking place, a sure sign your immune system is battling to protect you. So the sickness, in a lot of ways, actually depicts the healthy fight of your immune system.

In normal cases, the invaders are banished from the body after the skirmish. With the coast clear, immune cells are so disciplined they die off. Some security cells and systems go back to their posts to prepare for the next challenge. By now, cells called macrophages have come in as a clean-up crew of sorts to pick up the debris and transmit information about the invaders, so your body will remember what they look like to be identified at a future date.

Now, the immune system isn't perfect by any means. Pathogens like bacteria and viruses can slip through the cracks of the defense systems. Or there can be invaders our bodies aren't familiar with, so we're unable to fight them efficiently. To cope with the second situation, sometimes the immune system unleashes an indiscriminate massive attack that strikes both the virus and the body itself. This is an extreme case of balance going awry that could end up killing ourselves. And it's what happened with COVID-19.

It speaks to the bigger truth about immunity. Yes, we want to help you feel better when it comes to the common cold slugging you in the face. But we also want you to utilize techniques and tactics to help bolster your immune cells so they're better prepared for any invaders that try to steal or damage the goods from your biological factory.

THE WESTERN APPROACH TO COMMON INVADERS

PREVENTION: Washing hands, avoiding spreading germs (masks, distancing), flu shot (injection of weakened or simulated virus for the body to produce antibodies against the invader).

MEDICINAL TREATMENTS: Antibiotics for bacterial infections. Antivirals for viruses. Over-the-counter medication to quiet symptoms like sore throat, stuffy nose, and headache.

OTHER APPROACHES: Zinc lozenges, Vitamin D and C, lots of rest, and don't forget chicken soup with vegetables—a warm, rich food that's easy to digest with essential nutrients like glycosaminoglycans and possibly even growth factors from bone and meat.

TCM APPROACH TO COLDS

TCM has its own version of immunity, called Protective Qi. This is the all-mighty Qi putting on a defensive hat. Protective Qi is located and circulating at the exterior of the body, particularly at the openings where pathogens (evils) may gain entry, such as the sweat pores. It could also be the guard at the body's windows and doors, as well as the mucosa—a lining of cells located on the inner surface of the digestive and respiratory tract rich in immune cells. In TCM, Protective Qi is compared to a "golden shield." People who are deficient show a syndrome of Protective Qi Deficiency (PQD). Symptoms include susceptibility to cold and flu, spontaneous sweating (due to "loosening" of the sweat pore), aversion to cold and wind, and lethargy. If you're wondering if you have PQD, we have a DIY diagnostic tool in the Introduction.

Common cold happens at the nose—the "opening of Lung" (TCM term), or a window where one gets a peek of Lung. In TCM, the Lung controls breathing as well as sweating, two processes with similar roles to disperse from within. This is why Protective Qi is similar in nature to Lung Qi, and Lung deficiency would result in PQD.

Although the "common cold" in the West is known to be caused by rhinovirus and other viruses, the primary pathogen in a typical cold is Wind. TCM literally calls the common cold "injured by Wind." Since Wind is known for its fickleness, a cold often comes at a time when the weather is changing and symptoms are acute. Wind is accompanied often by Cold or Heat. A common cold is mainly differentiated as Wind-Cold Syndrome (without a fever) or Wind-Heat Syndrome (with a fever and sometimes expectoration).

TCM FOR Y-O-U

Immunity involves a complex number of factors that are different for everyone. And immune boosters can come in a variety of forms. Enhance yours with these strategies.

HERBAL THERAPY

TCM has a category of herbs specialized in fighting the Wind, among which ginger root and Gegeng (Pueraria lobota) are the most well known. Nonetheless, treatment differs depending on the syndrome differentiation. Wind-Cold syndrome requires herbs with a warming property—sweating in this case would help expel the Cold factors. Whereas Wind-Heat syndrome requires something with a cooling property.

Since PQD is a serious predisposing factor, strengthening Protective Qi is a major preventive measure. TCM has a classic formula just for this purpose, YuPinFeng (Jade Screen Powder). It features astragalus, a well-known Qi-enhancing herb that also helps to reinforce the body surface, such as closing down the sweat pores. It serves as the "king" ingredient of the formula.

FOOD THERAPY TO BOOST IMMUNITY

FROM YOUR BELLY...	TO YOUR BODY
Lingzhi (reishi mushroom)	A household TCM herb for enhancing Qi that's rich in beta-glucan, a natural compound known to boost immunity against Cold and other conditions of upper respiratory tract infection
Radish	Works by clearing away Heat, detoxifying the body, and dispelling (or preventing) the pathogen Cold—cut up a sweet and juicy radish, press out a ½ cup of juice, then mash a slice of ginger. Combine ginger and radish juice and a bit of sugar or honey with a cup of boiling water and mix well. Drink three times a day
Ginger black tea	The Wind-Cold element is associated with headaches, nasal congestion, runny nose, joint pain, and other symptoms—combine brown sugar, ginger tea, black tea, and hot water. Drink once or twice a day to warm the body and expel Cold

SELF-MASSAGE TO ENHANCE YOUR IMMUNITY

WHERE	ACU POINT	TCM THEORY	WHAT TO DO	LOCATE IT
Base of your thumbs	Yuji	This area is closely related to the respiratory Organs	Rub together the thenar eminence muscles at the base of your thumbs on your palms. Massaging each side for two minutes daily can improve cold symptoms	
Sides of your nose	Yingxiang	This area has special pressure points that can help with relieve symptoms like nose congestion	Clench your fists and massage the two sides of your nose with the back of your flexed thumbs 100 times each day	

CHAPTER 12

BEAUTY AND THE EAST

THE THREAT: *Declines in Skin Health*
THE TCM SYMBOLIC ORGAN: *Heart and others*
THE MISSION OF THE EAST-WEST ALLIANCE: *Look Better, Feel Better, Be Healthier*

As a kid, you probably only thought about your skin when something bad happened—a scraped knee, a sunburned back, a sibling who pinched you during quiet time hoping you'd squeal like a pack of piglets and get into some serious trouble.

In your teens, as you grew more self-aware, your skin meant much more. Pimples ruined days. Makeup took time. And yesterday's mirror was today's phone—you spent more time in front of it than anything else.

Early on and throughout your life, you knew your looks mattered. Research confirms what we inherently know—appearance plays a leading role in relationships, job prospects, and overall happiness.

Of course we know what's on the inside matters more than what's on the outside (cue Hallmark card), but we shouldn't discount the role of beauty when it comes to health for a couple of reasons:

» The health of your skin (and your hair to a lesser extent) are a proxy for your overall health. That is, when bad stuff is happening on your outer layer, there's a good chance something bad is also happening on the inside. And vice versa. Healthy skin shows your machinery on the inside may be working well too. Skin isn't just a symbol, it's a manifestation of biological processes going on in your body.

» Looks influence how you feel. If you're noticing dry skin, lackluster hair, blemishes, wrinkles, or other indicators of aging or poor skin, it may have something to do with other systems of your body—and come out in the form of stress, anxiety, depression, and more.

» Some skin conditions (whether they're acute or chronic) are more than just vanity issues. They're health problems in and of themselves, and many of them can be treated with TCM techniques (see specific conditions in Part 4).

So as you think about a youthful, vibrant appearance, don't get trapped into feeling like it's your ego masquerading as health. It is indeed part of your overall approach to health and wellness—and a major one at that.

Western medicine has many products and approaches for improving your skin (and we do like many of them), but it's also worth looking at what TCM offers to see where you can add sparkle and shine to make your outside as healthy as your insides.

THAT'S A WRAP:
The Biology of Skin Health

We spend a lot of time thinking about the exteriors in our life—the phone case we want, what color to paint our house, the clothes we wear.

At first glance, these exteriors may seem like they're all about style—what a color or design says about you. That's certainly true (as any bedazzled phone-case-carrying tween will attest). But they also serve a major function of protection—a case to protect your phone, paint as a first layer of defense against weather, clothes to shield you from the elements (and anti-nudity laws).

Your skin is no different. As your body's largest organ and biological form of wrapping paper, it ultimately serves the purpose to protect you from toxins and threats (like too much sun). Similar to the shingles on a house, our skin survives elements every day. The difference is, unlike the roof that needs replacing every 20 years, your skin renews itself every month or so. That's how rough skin can turn smooth in just a few weeks. Some changes, however, are more difficult to reverse, such as wrinkles and speckles. They're a reflection of our nutrition, endocrine, immune, and nervous systems, and are part of the aging process.

To keep skin healthy, you must protect all of its layers:

>> **Epidermis:** This thin, top layer not only serves as the outermost cover for protection, it also contains cells that play a special role in the function of your immune system.
>> **Dermis:** This middle layer is responsible for a lot of what happens in your body. It's where sweat glands and nerve endings are found, where hair grows, and where blood vessels make way for your body to provide nutrients to the skin.
>> **Subcutaneous fat:** Fat storage area to help protect your bones, keep you warm, and assist blood vessel function.

Your skin is made up of proteins—collagen, elastin, and keratin—which give it toughness and flexibility and serve as the main protectors against damage. As they begin to lose their function, you start to see signs of aging, such as wrinkles.

Keeping your skin healthy comes down to two main approaches—shielding it from the sun's harmful UV radiation to protect against cancers and sun damage, and nourishing it the right way (with water and other key vitamins and minerals, and beneficial molecules).

THE WESTERN APPROACH TO SKIN HEALTH

PREVENTION: Though some sun exposure without sun block to your torso and extremities is recommended to get a daily dose of Vitamin D (about 15 minutes per day, depending on skin color); any time longer requires using sun protection products with a SPF 30 or higher. This helps to minimize or prevent sun damage. (The 15-minute limit applies even when it's cold outside, shirtless Packers fans!)

SURGICAL: With sun damage that's precancerous or cancerous, various techniques are used to remove the suspect spots. Regular checks help minimize long-term damage.

PRODUCTS: Supplements like antioxidants (vitamins E, selenium, etc.) help fight UV damage, omega-3 fatty oils support the skin barrier that keeps the skin hydrated, Vitamin C is part of collagen synthesis and helps in skin healing. Retinols, which force the skin to rejuvenate itself, are the most common medical treatment recommended by dermatologists. Medications are also used with skin conditions such as acne or eczema.

THE TCM APPROACH

Since "outer beauty" encompasses so many areas of the body (skin, hair, nails, and lips), and beauty is sustained by inner health, it's no surprise various aspects of beauty correspond to different Organs. If you recall, TCM Organs are defined under the Force of Five, and here's how it plays out:

Heart = face
Lung = skin
Kidney = hair
Liver = nails
Spleen = lips

Among the five beauty areas, the face gets top bidding. Its rich expressiveness reflects one's Spirit (mental activity) governed by Heart (it is not only the heart organ from Western medicine). Therefore, a lackluster face accompanied by low Spirit may come from Heart Qi deficiency. What's more, according to TCM, the face is where all meridians converge—it's a complex place that could reflect the status of Heart as well as other Organs.

Armed with the above theory, here's how a TCM doctor sees a cosmetics patient in a clinic:

> » Lackluster face accompanied by low Spirit = Heart Qi deficiency
> » Yellow-tinted face, pale and dry lips, accompanied by lethargy and obesity = Spleen Qi deficiency
> » Brittle hair and dry, rough skin = Lung deficiency
> » Hair loss and sunken cheeks = Kidney Yin deficiency
> » Pale, bloated face accompanied by loss of shine in the eyes = Kidney Yang deficiency
> » Dark complexion with speckles and freckles = stagnation of Qi and Blood

TCM maps outer beauty to inner health, much different from the systemic control by hormones (especially estrogen, testosterone, and glucocorticoids) in Western medicine. Treatment is tailored to each individual and can include massage, nutrition, meditation, acupuncture, herbs, and exercise—with some therapies achieving long-lasting, whole-body results.

TCM FOR Y-O-U

With so many products and promises surrounding skincare, it's hard to know what may be most effective. The following methods have long been used by Eastern cultures to help address damaged skin and preserve a youthful radiance.

FOOD THERAPY TO MAKE YOUR SKIN GLOW

FROM YOUR BELLY...	TO YOUR BODY
Black sesame, walnut	Grind 1 Tbsp. of each and add to porridge every morning
Carrot, celery, apple, and blueberry juice	Beneficial for any skin condition—in case of skin rashes, daily consumption is recommended during a flare up, and once or twice weekly while in remission or a maintenance method

SELF-MASSAGE TO SAVE YOUR SKIN

WHERE	ACU POINT	TCM THEORY	WHAT TO DO	LOCATE IT
On speckles/ dark spots	N/A	Likely through enhancing Blood movement and expelling the toxins	Stretch the thumb and bend the other four fingers to press the center of a sizable speckle with the tip of the thumb—with pressure exerted perpendicular to the skin, gradually and steadily increase the strength, until it reaches the dermis	

On wrinkles	N/A	Likely through enhancing local Blood movement and hence reducing Blood stasis	Rub around the temples or take your middle and ring fingers and rub above and below the eye from the center of the face outward	
On all skin conditions	N/A	Promote local skin Qi movement and provide nutrients	Apply bergamot, lavender, rose oil, or tea tree oil to the affected area—do so after the skin is cleaned	

DIY Facial Masks

Qibaisan is a common prescription for a topical whitening formula in TCM. It's made up of seven kinds of Traditional Chinese medicinals. Its main function is to lighten freckles and remove acne.

1. Prepare equal parts of these seven ingredients:
   1. Ampelopsis root
   2. Bighead atractylodes rootstalk
   3. Pharbitidis seed
   4. White peony root
   5. White batryticated silkworm
   6. Angelica dahurica root
   7. Angelica Sinensis

2. Grind ingredients into a powder
3. Mix with honey, egg white, and/or milk to make a paste
4. Apply to skin and leave on for 10-15 minutes
5. Wash off with water

FOR BLEMISHED SKIN:

1.   Apply raw honey, tea of dandelion, or golden-seal root to fresh watermelon rind (the white skin part)
2.   Rub coated rind over cleansed skin
3.   Apply as a facial mask for 30 minutes
4.   Rinse off with warm water

FOR RASH:

1.   Apply sliced cucumber to the rash-affected area of face
2.   Let sit for 30 minutes
3.   Rinse with filtered water
4.   Gently pat coconut oil over face as a final touch

FOR WRINKLE TREATMENT:

Method 1:

1.   Pearl powder ⅛ tsp., ½ mashed banana, and 2 Tbsp milk
2.   Mix well
3.   Apply to face
4.   Wash off with water

Method 2:

1.   Pearl powder ⅛ tsp., and 2 egg whites
2.   Mix well
3.   Apply to skin for 15–20 minutes
4.   Wash off with water

Method 3: Good for both acne-blemished skin and reducing wrinkles

1.   Pearl powder ⅛ tsp., and aloe flesh (mashed)
2.   Mix well
3.   Apply to face for 30 minutes
4.   Wash off with water

Method 4: Helps both wrinkles and acne

1.   Prepare ½ Tbsp paste of bentonite and cucumber (grated)
2.   Moisten with apple cider vinegar
3.   Apply to face for 30 minutes
4.   Wash off with warm water

Hair and There

Your skin isn't the only outward signal of your health. Luscious locks and bouncy curls do more than just attract attention—they provide protection from the sun, while also being symbolic of your inner health. In TCM, doctors use various foods to treat a variety of hair problems.

» As hair is governed by Kidney that corresponds to the color black, hair loss may call for black foods like sesame or mushroom.

TCM also uses topical formulas to help treat oily hair and associated hair loss. Leaves similar to cypress leaves are used in this process:*

1. Prepare fresh wild arborvitae leaves
2. Wrap in gauze
3. Place about 16 oz. of arborvitae leaves in 9 cups of water (the amount can be adjusted according to use)
4. Clarify the water by bringing it to a boil
5. Apply to hair and wash out without shampoo

*Although their leaves look very similar—both are evergreen coniferous trees with flattened shoots bearing small scale-like leaves—the medicinal difference between arborvitae leaves and cypress leaves is huge! Cypress has leaves in four rows, branches are round and somewhat pliable, while arborvitae leaves are always opposite and sometimes have a raised gland on the back.

A Note About Cosmetic Acupuncture

Acupuncture provides a safe, natural, and effective way to achieve cosmetic results. It clears the Qi and Blood channels that are jammed during aging, and is believed in TCM to be effective in combating sagging skin and wrinkles. Needles are placed at strategic meridian energy points in the body. The number of needles depends on the individual's overall physical condition and the size of the area being treated. Although one session can make a quick difference, up to 10 sessions (over a five- or six-week period) are needed to achieve a longer-lasting effect. You'll begin to look younger and feel better, without the worry of harmful toxins injected into your body—or the risks of surgery. Most importantly, your overall health may be improved—deeper sleep, better digestion, mentally feel calmer, and more energetic.

CHAPTER 13

FEEL ZAPPED?
ADD ZIP!

THE THREAT: *Fatigue*
THE TCM SYMBOLIC ORGAN: *Spleen, Kidney*
THE MISSION OF THE EAST-WEST ALLIANCE: *Energize Your Body
to Energize Your Life*

Life comes at you fast. Sometimes, even when you *want* to handle it all—work, family, stress, to-do lists, trying to keep up with Aunt Jennie's Facebook rants, societal angst—you just can't seem to muster up the strength. It's no surprise many of us suffer from a severe case of "can't we just go back to bed?" (Add in a pandemic that has likely tested your resilience and will too, and many days you've probably felt like an unlucky salmon on the wrong end of a bear jaw).

Fatigue is one of those medical words that—clinically speaking—is abstract, in that there's no one cause or cure. But in practical terms, it's far from abstract. In fact, it's more concrete than a sidewalk. Your body aches, you don't have the gumption to get up and go, and the last thing you feel like doing is, well, *everything*.

Without overstating its significance, it's clear we have a serious fatigue problem. What we wouldn't give to be built a little like a car—turn a key to start, press the gas to go as fast as you want, tap the brakes when you need a break, then turn the key to wind down. Our bodies, of course, don't work like that. It's more like an orchestra of hormones and chemicals all playing different instruments to create your energy concerto.

For many of us, a lot is out of tune and we don't quite know how to get everything in sync. Instead, we rely on outside forces to provide our energy. #CoffeeMemes

And while there's nothing terribly wrong with some amount of caffeine or other kinds of energy boosters, the bigger question is: How can we energize and optimize our own bodies, rather than relying on a quadruple-shot-espresso latté?

Addressing fatigue isn't easy—it's complex with many variables—but that's why TCM can be an excellent place to turn. A whirlwind of technological advances has led us to believe fatigue is a modern-day phenomenon, but the truth is fatigue is inherently *human*. And TCM has addressed this issue for thousands of years through its own remedies and approaches. So if Western medicine hasn't helped you find and fix your slow motor, it's worth looking into some other approaches.

After all, an active life is the source for happiness.

If you have low or no energy, you're more likely to turn to unhealthy habits (this doughnut will make me feel better!) or not engage in healthy habits (who has the juice to exercise when you can barely muster the energy to tie your shoes?).

But when the situation is flipped—when you feel good, when you feel alive, when you feel like you could chug and churn and grind and go—a healthy version of dominos is created. You eat better, you exercise more, you sleep soundly, and you *feel* better. So as we look at the components of fatigue, know this: Your energy issues aren't unusual, and though they may be frustrating, you can take steps to make a difference and live the life you want.

WIRED TO BE TIRED:
The Biology of Fatigue

In the old days when you would say you were tired the prescription was simple and direct—get more sleep. Through the years, we've learned fatigue is not quite so simple. In fact, it's complex. Countless possible causes and sources are leading you to zombie your way through life. And to pinpoint those trigger points for every person isn't easy. It could be anything (and multiple things) causing your low energy. (We're talking about chronic forms of fatigue—not just the occasional zapped feeling you have from time to time).

For many people, it means you and your doctors are your own mad scientists tinkering with medications or lifestyle changes to find your own special energy-boosting formula. We can get clues from some diagnostics—blood tests may reveal low hormone or iron levels—but it doesn't always tell the whole story.

Biologically, energy comes from mitochondria in your cells—basically a cell's power plant to generate the energy it uses to function—that fuel your body. We don't think much about mitochondria in our day-to-day lives (i.e. man, I need a mito boost!), but some of your fatigue may be linked to some kind of mitochondria dysfunction. And frequently, the burner/mito is switched off, or its fuel line is cut, due to endocrine anomalies such as insulin resistance. When the mitochondria are sluggish, so are you.

In general terms, we do know fatigue issues fall into two categories. In both cases, fatigue fiddles with your internal systems and cells to alter your sleep or disrupt normal cellular functions that affect energy levels.

YOUR LIFESTYLE: There's clear evidence many aspects play a role in energy—how your cells and Organs get the power they need to run efficiently and effectively. Unsurprisingly, they fall into the four big health categories:

> » *Nutrition*: Blood sugar levels directly affect how you feel. Eating simple carbs that are high in sugar gives you spikes in blood glucose that quickly fall, causing your energy levels to roller

coaster all day. High sugar and high fat diets can also cause mitochondrial stress. Balanced diets of healthy fats and carbs and lean sources of protein create steady energy, suppling a slow drip, rather than a guzzle of glucose.

» *Activity:* Staying physically active, including regular exercise, fortifies your muscles, cardiovascular system, and other areas to improve energy. A sedentary lifestyle makes your metabolism slow and sluggish, further bringing out your inner sloth.

» *Sleep:* It stands to reason, if you don't get restorative sleep, you feel tired. A lack of sleep disrupts the natural repair process your cells and Organs need to stay fine-tuned to perform at their best.

» *Mind and Mood:* Stress, anxiety, depression, and other head-hurters also affect energy-supporting hormone levels.

YOUR MEDICAL CONDITIONS: All of the above may seem straightforward to you. Eat well, exercise regularly, get some sleep—*voila!*—you'll feel better. But we all know it's not quite that easy. Other things may be going on in your body that are not only impacting how you feel, but also influencing your ability to engage in healthy behaviors.

The Mayo Clinic lists more than two dozen medical conditions that can be a source of fatigue—everything from pervasive conditions like obesity, diabetes, anemia, thyroid disease, and heart disease to more specific problems like concussions and inflammatory bowel disease. And we haven't even gotten the natural hormonal changes with aging or the obscure infections that are just being discovered. So it's no wonder why sources of fatigue are so difficult to pinpoint.

Diagnostic tools are available that can help. For example, doctors will often look at key markers—thyroid, iron, vitamin B12—to see if supplementation or medication may work.

So, is it really a matter of medical sleuthing? In most cases, yes, there's no one easy answer. It's also difficult to look at fatigue as a holistic problem that needs a three-dimensional approach. But that's truly the key—your answer is likely not one answer, but a few pieces put together to help you feel like you can rev your body's engine whenever you want.

THE WESTERN APPROACH TO FATIGUE

For the most frequent cases, fatigue is often not diagnosed with a specific cause but lumped together as chronic fatigue syndrome. For people in this category, there's no proven cure or even effective treatments.

SUPPLEMENTS AND MEDICATIONS: Doctors will often suggest supplements such as B Vitamins or iron to help boost energy. Thyroid medication can help regulate the energy-related thyroid hormone. And if you suffer from symptoms associated with fatigue, like depression, pain, or diabetes, solving these problems can also have an effect on fatigue.

HORMONES: A comprehensive profile of all your hormones—especially estrogen, progesterone, and testosterone—is imperative. A bioidentical hormones prescription may be recommended. Doctors may also search for obscure microbiome infections.

LIFESTYLE: Diet, exercise, and sleep hygiene are key recommendations for trying to calm the body for restorative rest and provide sustained energy levels throughout the day. It's not surprising that TCM doctors also recommend avoiding rich, greasy foods and eating healthy foods for sustained energy.

THE TCM APPROACH

Although fatigue as a disease was not defined by the Center for Disease Control of USA until 1988, TCM recognized this illness in the classic literature more than 2,000 years ago. In it, fatigue is considered as deficiencies of Yin, Yang, Qi, and Blood. The theories and therapies of TCM for fatigue are sophisticated, primarily due to a long history of clinical experience. The stress on Yin-Yang balance gives TCM a sensitive edge in addressing health issues undetectable to Western instruments, making TCM especially appropriate for dealing with fatigue.

Major TCM fatigue syndromes with fatigue associated symptoms include:

> **Spleen Qi deficiency**: Poor appetite, slight abdominal distention, loose stools—this accounts for the lion's share of fatigue cases.
> **Lung Qi deficiency**: Low voice, not willing to speak, chronic dry cough, spontaneous sweating, susceptibility to cold.
> **Kidney Yang deficiency**: Fear of cold, prefer hot food and drink, sore and weak lumbar and legs, frequent urination, lack of sexual desire.
> **Heart Blood deficiency**: Palpitation, pale face, insomnia, dizziness, blurred vision, numbness in limbs, menstrual irregularities.
> **Liver Qi stagnation**: Stomachache, blurred vision, dry eyes, cramping.

You see from the above pathologies, fatigue, like other problems, is all about Yin-Yang balance, as shown by the key words "deficiency" and "stagnation." In other words, fatigue is such a big and whole-body disruption it takes a holistic remedy to restore balance. However, what's interesting is TCM doctors will also do their own sleuthing to figure out what Organ to best address in the remedies. The TCM Organ presents itself in a very distinct way compared to that of Western medicine—as a facet of all-encompassing Qi. Sounds familiar, right? Recall what we said about TCM Organs in Chapter 4, and in Chapter 5 the process of syndrome differentiation at the center of a TCM doctors' thinking as they analyze you using the "ancient TCM code."

TCM doctors will look for ailments that pair with fatigue to determine the treatment. Common co-symptoms include changes in hair, bone pain, loss of sex drive, tinnitus, or hearing problems. As they identify you with a syndrome, they know how the balance is tipped and where it happens, thus giving them the best formula to treat your fatigue. In all of these cases, though, the main driver is restoring the flow of Qi and Yin-Yang balance.

TCM FOR Y-O-U

When it comes to restoring Yin-Yang balance, TCM has special age-old approaches. There are specific formulas for invigorating Yang, nourishing Yin, invigorating Qi, and enriching Blood. In practice, the treatment varies depending on the affected Organs and other individual conditions. In addition, acupuncture, massage, Qigong, and other therapies also work on fatigue.

FOOD THERAPY FOR FIGHTING FATIGUE

FROM YOUR BELLY...	TO YOUR BODY
Millet, sweet potato, Chinese yam, dates, pumpkin, orange peels, astragalus	These foods all help with Spleen deficiency to help fight fatigue—find recipes with these ingredients, or add them to your meals as you see fit
Ginseng	Widely heralded for its ability to strengthen and bolster Qi—different varieties of ginseng can suit people with different needs—for instance, Asian ginseng has warming qualities and is ideal for those who tend to feel cold and out of breath, hence better suited for treating fatigue
Goji berry	Replenishes vital Essence and Yin, nourishes Blood and Jing fluid, tonifies Liver and Kidney Yin

SELF-MASSAGE TO ADD SPUNK

WHERE	ACU POINT	TCM THEORY	WHAT TO DO	LOCATE IT
The tip of the thumb when it's placed over the webbing between the thumb and pointer finger of the other hand, with the thumb's traverse skin line right on the web's edge	Hegu	Helps to clear the flow of Qi	Knead the point of the left hand in a rotating manner with the thumb of the right hand for 2-3 minutes to feel soreness—switch the left and right hands and repeat the above actions	
Top of the scalp	Baihui	Helps improve mental functions, calms nerves, and promotes flow of Qi	Press and rub the area for five minutes and repeat multiple times each day	

PART 4

A GUIDE TO TCM TREATMENTS

MAKE A MOTION

☯

A Guide to Musculoskeletal Pain

When it comes to pain, an overarching TCM principle applies: "Where there is pain, there's blockage" (or impediment). Most orthopedic pains are attributed to one defined TCM condition: impediment disorder. This is a condition largely caused by three pathogens that present themselves in a trio: Wind, Cold, and Dampness, although the predominant pathogen or pathogens may differ case by case. Dampness and Cold block the running of Qi and Blood, whereas Wind moves pain around in the body or turns it on and off.

In TCM, musculoskeletal tissues have a tissue-specific connection with the Organs. For instance, Liver "governs" the tendons and ligaments, Spleen "governs" the muscles, and Kidney "governs" the bones. Here governance means nourishment and protection from pathogens.

Common practices:

» Stay away from cold and damp places.
» Use a heating pad to remove the Cold pathogen.
» Employ foods as medication. Cinnamon powder, turmeric powder, and ginger are good to warm the body. Bean sprouts, red bean, tofu, Coix seed, and winter melon (wax gourd) are beneficial for expelling Dampness.

LOWER BACK PAIN

Lower back pain is one of the most common complaints in the United States and other countries. It comes as you get older, starting at around age 30 or 40. Muscle strain and other injuries—herniated discs (sciatica), inflammation such as arthritis and tendonitis, and other kinds of pain—are often treated with physical therapy, medication, even surgical procedures.

The soft tissue of the waist is susceptible to pulling and squeezing, which leads to damage and degeneration. Improper posture or long-term force can lead to chronic strain of soft tissue in the lower back. External forces can cause ligament tearing around the small spinal joints, joint damage, and intervertebral disc dislocation or protrusion. In addition, kidney lesions and women's pelvis pain can often radiate to the waist and cause low back pain.

In TCM, chronic lower back ache typically starts from Kidney deficiency, including Kidney Yin deficiency (often characterized by dry throat and insomnia) and Kidney Yang deficiency (often characterized by cold feet and hands). This deficiency is further complicated by the invasion of Wind, Cold, and Dampness. Cold would cause muscle constraint, while Dampness would cause Qi stagnation. These reasons would lead to chronic lower back ache.

SELF-MASSAGE

SHENSHU MASSAGE: This maneuver is good
for detoxification (expelling the pathogens).

1. Locate the spine bone at the navel level
   and move to either side by 2 fingers'
   width
2. Heat up both hands by quickly rubbing
   your palms together (Mr. Miyagi style)
3. Rub both hands up and down on the
   Shenshu point
4. Massage 1 to 2 times a day, 3–5 minutes each time

YONGQUAN MASSAGE: Particularly effective for strengthening
Kidney Yin

1. Immerse your feet in warm water for a few
   minutes
2. Sit with your legs crossed and the sole of
   each foot facing upwards
3. Locate YongQuan point located in the
   center of your sole
4. Press and knead 100 times with the
   thumb longwise to your foot

HERBAL & FOOD REMEDIES

In TCM, different foods are used to ease lower back pain. Look for recipes
with these powerful, deficiency–busting ingredients in our recipe section:

KIDNEY YANG DEFICIENCY: Use walnut, cinnamon powder,
cayenne pepper, and chive seed.

KIDNEY YIN DEFICIENCY: Consider bitter melon, tremella, lily
bulb, goji berry, and mulberry.

NECK AND SHOULDER PAIN

Neck and shoulder pain has increased exponentially with the widespread use of computers and smartphones. The problem, apart from the muscle pain you might experience, is it may also lead to issues like dizziness, headaches, and other symptoms. This can stem from muscle strain, nerve compression due to disc herniation and other causes, inflammation such as arthritis, and tendonitis, trauma, and more.

In TCM, the root cause is impediment syndrome, often associated with deficiency in Liver, Kidney, Qi, and Blood.

SELF-MASSAGE

FENGCHI MASSAGE

1. Press your thumbs firmly underneath the base of your skull into the hollow areas on both sides
2. Close your eyes and slowly tilt your head back
3. Breathe deeply and press up from underneath the skull for one to two minutes

JIANJING MASSAGE

1. Locate the midpoint between the most prominent spine bone at the base of the neck and the edge of your shoulders
2. Grasp and release 20-30 times each side

HERBAL & FOOD REMEDIES

In TCM, different foods are used to treat neck and shoulder pain. Carrot, celery, and apple juice can nourish pain-related Organs and tissues to build up strong muscles, bones, and sinews. Common kitchen seasonings turmeric, cinnamon, fennel, and cayenne powder are known for their anti-inflammation and pain-relief properties. Find recipes with these powerful ingredients, along with our favorite pain-relieving Geng-Ciwujia Congee recipe, in our recipes section.

JOINT PAIN / ARTHRITIS

Joint pain is a major symptom of arthritis. Arthritis has different types—osteoarthritis, rheumatic, rheumatoid, etc.—and each affects joints differently. Depending on the form and severity, treatments can include anti-inflammatory medications and joint replacement surgery. In TCM, arthritis manifests primarily as impediment syndrome. In fact, rheumatic arthritis in Chinese literally means arthritis of "Wind and Dampness." Heat is also sometimes present in patients with Yin deficiency.

SELF-MASSAGE

KNEE MASSAGE: For knee arthritis, massaging specific acupuncture points (see table below) for 2–3 minutes each is a gentle way to ease pain.

PRESSURE POINT	LOCATION	
Liangqiu:	When you stretch your knees, the hollow where the muscles protrude	
Shuangxiyan:	Sit down with your knees bent 90 degrees, place hands on top of the knees, on each knee, use your thumb and index finger to look for the inner and outer depressions—there are two acupoints on each knee	
Xuehai:	Straighten your legs, there will be a depression on the inside of your knees. There is a raised muscle above the depression, notice the top of the muscle is Xuehai acupoint	

HERBAL & FOOD REMEDIES

In TCM, different foods are used to treat neck joint pain and arthritis. Yi Ren (Coix seed), cinnamon, and turmeric powders are commonly used as therapy ingredients for their pain-relieving properties. Find recipes with these powerful ingredients, along with our favorite porridge recipes (Longan and Bean Porridge and Cinnamon Porridge), in our recipes section.

GOUT

Gout, a special type of arthritis, is caused by the disorder of uric acid metabolism, hence the accumulation of uric acid in the blood and tissues. It's associated with recurrent inflammation in joints of the lower limbs, most often at either side of the joint where the big toe joins the sole.

In TCM, gout is attributed to the pathogens of Dampness and Phlegm. Heat is often a factor, especially at the time of acute flare.

HERBAL & FOOD REMEDIES

In TCM, different foods are used to treat the different phases of gout. Look for these favorite soup recipes, along with others with the same powerful, flare–busting ingredients, in our recipe section:

CHRONIC PHASE: Red Bean and Sponge Gourd Vein Soup

ACUTE PHASE: Papaya and Rengdongteng (Casulis Lonicerae) Soup

MUSCLE PAIN / FIBROMYALGIA

Chronic muscle pain often comes from fibromyalgia syndrome. The exact cause is unknown, and Western medicine has yet to find an effective therapy for this elusive syndrome, other than temporarily relieving the symptoms. It's associated with dull and lasting muscle pain, often accompanied by irritable bowel syndrome, anxiety, depression, and fatigue.

TCM considers this condition under impediment syndrome, sometimes complicated by accumulation of phlegm and stasis of Blood, which results in lasting pain.

MOVEMENT THERAPY

QIGONG: To ease muscle pain, practice for 15 minutes once each day. Learn more about QiGong on page 73.

1. Sit or lie down in a quiet room
2. Focus on the Guanyuan point four fingers' width under your navel
3. Breathe in, hold, then slowly breathe out
4. Repeat this inhale and exhale pattern, making sure each breath is deep and slow

IT'S ALL IN YOUR HEAD:
Conditions Associated with the Head

The head is an epicenter of your body. It's complexity means a lot can happen inside—from run-of-the-mill aches to much more severe issues and consequences. With so much at stake, we take head problems seriously.

That's not only because it's the site of the brain, but also because meridians channel through the head—meaning every function of the body funnels through the head, according to TCM. No one part your anatomy is isolated, there's a connection to the head in almost every condition. That's why ear seeding works for a host of ailments all around the body, and a peek at the face allows doctors to tell stories of inside Organs.

Aside from the meridians, the head is also the "world expo" of the internal Organs with its "five orifices", eye, tongue, mouth, nose, and ear. Each serves as a window through which doctors glean insight into your Organ's status. That is, eye for the Liver, tongue for the Heart, mouth for the Spleen, nose for the Lung, and ear for the Kidney. It's why, for instance, when you start to have an annoying ringing in ear your TCM doctor gives you a prescription to enhance your Kidney.

HEADACHE

As you know from your experience with Western medicine, headaches can be tricky. Finding a cause or source may seem almost endless. It's no different in TCM. There can be external causes like Wind, Cold, Dampness, and Heat, and there can be internal ones, too. Various kinds of problems in the human body can cause headaches. All the meridians converging on the head is one of the most important reasons. Depression, anger, and long-term mental stress could also cause headache. Here's how TCM approaches headaches:

TCM THEORY	SYMPTOM	CAUSE
Liver fire flames up to disturb brain function	The pain—along with dizziness, restlessness, irritability, mood swings, or rib aches—gets worse the longer it lasts. Symptoms may include yellow fur-coated tongue and bitter taste in the mouth	Stress due to work overload, poor lifestyle choices like overindulging with alcohol or cigarettes, lack of sound sleep, staying up late
Deficiency of both Qi and Blood (the brain lacks nourishment)	Dull pain, fatigue, pale face, pale and enlarged tongue	Nutrition deficiency, work overload, lack of sleep
Blood stasis (possible injury prior to the pain)	Stubborn, sharp pain always affects the same area of head, history of head injury, deep red tongue	Injury, lack of physical activity, cardiovascular conditions
Kidney Qi weakness (brain lacks Kidney Qi support)	Sense of emptiness, dizzy, lower back pain, weakness in both legs, red tongue with no coating	Sexual indulgence, emotional excess (fear, anxiety, etc.), chronic diseases, aging
Dampness	Headache with the sense of heaviness, lots of mucus or phlegm in the mouth or throat, dizziness, tongue coated with thick white fur	Excessive sweets, greasy or cold foods, Spleen Qi deficiency

SELF-MASSAGE

» **FENGCHI:**

1. Firmly press your thumbs underneath the base of your skull into the hollow areas on both sides.

2. With eyes closed, slowly tilt your head back and press up from underneath the skull for one to two minutes, breathe deeply.

» **TEMPLES:** Rub a drop of lavender oil into temples to relieve pain. If the pain is around the eyes, do the same around eyebrows for two minutes.

» **HEGU:** Place half of the right thumb over the webbing between the thumb and point finger of the left hand, with the thumb's traverse skin line right on the web's edge. Knead in a rotating manner for 2–3 minutes to feel soreness. Switch hands and repeat.

COMPLETE HEAD MASSAGE:

1. Heat up both hands by quickly rubbing your palms together (Mr. Miyagi style)
2. Gently massage your whole head starting at the top
3. Move down to massage both sides
4. Move forward to massage your forehead, eyes, cheeks, and jaw
5. Move to the back of your head and end at the base of your skull
6. Repeat 20 times, gradually increasing pressure

TOP OF SCALP:

1. Use your fingers to exert pressure on the top of your head
2. Repeat 20 to 30 times while gradually increasing the pressure

WATER THERAPY

HOT BATH: Before bedtime, take a hot bath to relax, relieve pain, and help to improve sleep.

HOT WATER FOOT SOAK: Also before sleep, soak both feet in hot water that's at least three inches over your ankles. Soak for 30–40 minutes, adding more hot water to keep the temperature very warm. The overall effect is the same as a hot bath.

MEDITATION THERAPY

QIGONG: To ease headache, practice for 30 minutes once each day. This daily meditation is not only brain relaxing and pain relieving, it also prevents reoccurring headaches. Learn more about QiGong on page 73.

1. Sit or lie down in a quiet room
2. Focus on the Guanyuan point four fingers' width under your navel
3. Breathe in, hold, then slowly breathe out
4. Repeat this inhale and exhale pattern, making sure each breath is deep and slow

HERBAL & FOOD REMEDIES

In TCM, different foods are used to ease headache symptoms and pain. See the Astragulus Congee with Lotus Seeds and Dates recipe on page 219. More of our favorite head-supporting recipes, ingredients, and teas include:

Chinese yam and goji berry congee: Good for all types of headache.
Walnut and sesame porridge: Quiets Kidney Qi weakness headache.
Bitter melon: Eases Liver fire headache.
Tianma: Relieves Dampness-caused headache.
Chamomile tea: Calms the head.
Peppermint tea: Clears Liver fire.
Valerian tea: Brings improved sleep and pain and tension relief.

Look for these recipes and more in our recipe section.

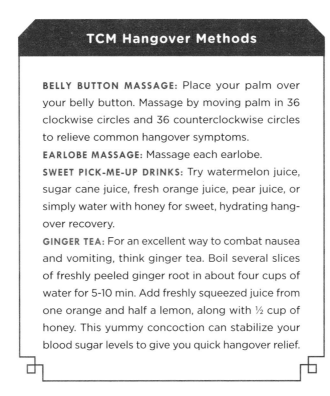

TCM Hangover Methods

BELLY BUTTON MASSAGE: Place your palm over your belly button. Massage by moving palm in 36 clockwise circles and 36 counterclockwise circles to relieve common hangover symptoms.

EARLOBE MASSAGE: Massage each earlobe.

SWEET PICK-ME-UP DRINKS: Try watermelon juice, sugar cane juice, fresh orange juice, pear juice, or simply water with honey for sweet, hydrating hang-over recovery.

GINGER TEA: For an excellent way to combat nausea and vomiting, think ginger tea. Boil several slices of freshly peeled ginger root in about four cups of water for 5-10 min. Add freshly squeezed juice from one orange and half a lemon, along with ½ cup of honey. This yummy concoction can stabilize your blood sugar levels to give you quick hangover relief.

TEMPOROMANDIBULAR JOINT DYSFUNCTION (TMD) / JAW PAIN

Jaw pain is often attributed to the dysfunction of the joint between the cheek bone and mandibular bone. Common symptoms include pain, swelling, and a lack of movement in or popping of the jaw. For TCM, the problem stems from systemic pathology—the flow of Qi at the superficial meridian or circulation of Blood. It's believed to occur due to the invasion of pathogens like Wind, Cold, and Dampness.

SELF-MASSAGE

TEMPLE AND JAWLINE MASSAGE: Two areas can be effective. One is directly above the ear to the temple, the other area is about 3 cm in front of the earlobe

1. Put a finger on either area of the two areas, and then open and close the mouth
2. When you close your mouth, gently bite your teeth together.
3. As the muscles contract and relax, you will feel the muscles jumping in and out
4. Place your thumb, index finger and middle finger on these areas and gently massage in small circles
5. Massage each point for 1 to 2 minutes to relax the tense muscles surrounding the joint

EAR RINGING (TINNITUS) / HEARING LOSS

Ear ringing and hearing loss are auditory disturbances caused by many kinds of diseases. Characterized by a ringing sound in the ears, the chirping of a cicada, or an ocean tide, it may be an indicator of the start of hearing loss.

In TCM, the ear is the orifice or opening of the Kidney. Tinnitus is a typical symptom of Kidney deficiency. We've talked in depth about this syndrome in the low libido chapter and how it is caused by insufficiency of Kidney Jing. This deficiency is often complicated by invasion of pathogens (Wind, Fire, and Dampness) that block running of Qi in the meridians that connect Kidney and ear, thereby further exacerbating the symptoms of tinnitus and hearing loss.

SELF-MASSAGE

Frequent stimulation of the reflex areas and acupuncture points on the ears can dredge the meridians and improve blood circulation.

1. PULL AND RUB EARS

With the thumb and index finger of both hands, respectively pinch the highest part of the auricle, the tip of the ear, and pull it upwards and let go. Repeat the strokes for 3-5 minutes. The intensity should not feel painful.

Then, rub the ears 30 times with the palms of both hands. End by rubbing the back of the ear 30 times.

2. MING TIAN DRUM

Put the palms of your hands close to the ears, tightly cover the ear holes with your palms, and stabilize them with your thumb and little finger. Use the other three fingers tap the occiput behind the head making the "dong-dong" sound in the ears like drumming. These three fingers correspond to three acupuncture points, namely Naohu, Fengfu, and Yamen.

HERBAL & FOOD REMEDIES

SYNDROME	SYMPTOMS	RECIPE
Liver fire flaming	Sudden deafness, tinnitus, headache, dizziness, red face, dry mouth, irritability, constipation, yellow urine	**Apple Bitter Gourd Juice:** Clearing away Heat and purging Fire, moistening the intestines, and a laxative effect. **Ingredients:** 1 bitter gourd, 1 apple, lemon juice, 1 tsp. of honey. **Directions:** 1. Wash the bitter gourd, remove the flesh, and cut into pieces. Wash the apple and cut into pieces. 2. Put bitter gourd and apple together in a blender, add cold water, and blend into a juice. 3. To serve, pour into a cup and add lemon juice and honey, to taste. Stir well.
Spleen weakness	Long-term stuffy unhealed ears, tinnitus, low tone, hearing loss, abdominal fullness, poor appetite, fatigue, loose stools	**Astragalus Porridge:** Replenish Qi and invigorate the Spleen. **Ingredients:** 30 g of Astragalus, ½ cup of glutinous rice. **Directions:** Cook the astragalus for 30–50 minutes. Remove the residue. Add glutinous rice to cook the porridge. Enjoy while hot.
Kidney Essence deficiency	Tinnitus (small cicadas), gradually worsening deafness, sleep more at night, dizziness, sore waist and knees	**Goji Chamomile Tea:** Nourish Liver and Kidney, clear deficiency Fire. **Ingredients:** 2 Tbsp. of goji berry, 3 Tbsp. of chamomile. **Directions:** Put ingredients in a thermos and add 2 cups of boiling water. Simmer for 30 minutes. Let cool before serving.
Qi stagnation and Blood stasis	Prolonged illness, tinnitus and deafness with dizziness and headache, irritability	**Hawthorn Astragalus Soup:** Stimulate waste elimination, invigorate QI, and activate Blood circulation **Ingredients:** 40 g hawthorn, 10 g astragalus, brown sugar. **Directions:** Smash the hawthorn. Mix all ingredients with water and make a decoction. Enjoy while warm.

SKIN IN THE GAME:
Major Skin Conditions

By TCM theory, the skin is the first barrier of protection for the body's internal Organs. At the same time, skin, nails, and hair are nourished by the inner Organs (see details in the "Beauty in the East" chapter). Inner Organs and exterior tissues are connected through meridian, Blood, and body fluids. Therefore, in TCM skincare takes a holistic approach. It's a story of "beauty from within." Any issues, including cosmetic issues, stem from the root problem of viscera, Qi, Blood, and body fluids.

ECZEMA

Eczema is a common skin problem characterized by an inflammatory condition of the skin. Symptoms include skin redness, itching, and vesicular lesions. Chronic eczema can make skin scaly, crusted, or hardened. TCM calls this condition "rash of Dampness." There are two common causes of eczema: deficiency of Spleen Qi, which results in internal Dampness; and invasion of external pathogens of Wind, Dampness, and Heat. Wind is characterized by acute flare, Heat by inflammation, and Dampness by blisters.

SELF-MASSAGE

FACIAL MASSAGE: Massage face in the morning and evening with a vitamin A-E emulsion and/or aloe gel. For oily skin, use cider vinegar.
NATURAL CLEANSING: Always use a natural soap to cleanse your skin. Avoid soap containing detergent to help clean the pores without irritation.

HERBAL & FOOD REMEDIES

In TCM, different foods are used to treat eczema. You are encouraged to enjoy foods recommended below, but avoid seafood and spicy food that invite Wind and Heat. Also avoid excessive eating behaviors that can harm the Spleen.

> **Astragalus:** The number one herb used as a Spleen Qi booster.
> **Lotus seed / Coix seed:** Both a food and also a traditional herb, they work to enhance the Spleen.

Mung bean / Honeysuckle flower / Portulaca / Dandelion: Often prescribed for eczema. They work to cleanse and detoxify (expel the pathogens). These herbs are also delicious foods in Chinese cooking and are safe and effective for long-term consumption.

ACNE

Acne is a skin condition that commonly occurs in adolescence. If not cared for, it can start at puberty and continue as a problem into adulthood. Severe acne can be both unsightly and painful, which can lead to physical and psychological consequences. Acne basically reflects hormone imbalance and malnutrition, while also being stress related.

In TCM, Heat is one of the primary causes of acne. Adolescence is a time when Yang Qi is at its peak. Robust Yang, if not balanced with Yin, can lead to Heat. That's why acne occurs mostly as a "curse" of adolescents. The face is the "venue where all Yangs meet" (as mentioned earlier), which explains why acne tends to show most in your complexion.

HERBAL & FOOD REMEDIES

In TCM, different foods are used to treat acne. The herbs used most often for acne flare ups and pain include: dandelion, mulberry leaf, bamboo leaf, and mung bean. Find our favorite recipe for congee for acne skin, along with many other powerful, breakout-reducing recipes, in the recipe section. Enjoy these foods and the others recommended below, but avoid spicy foods—they are Warming in nature.

Mung bean: Well-known food with Heat-clearing activity that is often cooked as a soup.

Royal jelly / Bee pollen / Maca: Recommended for acne patients who have mood swings and irregular menstruation. Each of these foods can effectively rebalance the hormone system, increase the body's resistance to infections, and reduce stress.

TOPICAL TREATMENTS

Carrot mask: Treatment to heal acne.

1. Cook and mash carrot
2. Let cool until warm
3. Thin carrot mash with organic whole milk to preferred consistency
4. Mix in a whisked egg yolk
5. Apply a thin layer to face
6. Rinse thoroughly with filtered water

Raw honey / Teas of dandelion / Goldenseal root rub: Good for blemished skin.

1. Apply ingredient of choice onto slices of fresh watermelon rind (the white skin part)
2. Massage coated peel over facial area
3. Rinse thoroughly with filtered water

Cucumber cure:

1. Apply sliced cucumber to the rashes / affected area of face
2. Leave on for 30 minutes
3. Rinse with filtered water
4. Press in coconut oil over face as the last touch

PSORIASIS

Psoriasis is a common, stubborn, chronic skin condition that affects about two percent of people in North America. It is prone to recurrence.

In TCM, psoriasis comes from three main pathologies: Blood-heat syndrome—bright-red lesion and rapid multiplying rashes; Blood dryness syndrome—dry scale and light-red lesion; and Blood stasis syndrome—dark-red and thickened lesion. Often the pathology is complicated by other factors, such as Dampness, Wind, and deficiency of Yin, Yang, or Blood.

HERBAL & FOOD REMEDIES

In TCM, different foods are used to treat psoriasis. Find our favorite recipe for psoriasis congee, along with many other powerful, lesion-reducing
recipes, in the recipe section. Recommended psoriasis foods revolve around
the three sub-type syndromes:

Blood cooling effect: Herbs like Shengdi (Rehmannia glutinosa), Danpi (Cortex moutan), and Xuansheng (Scrophularia
ningpoensis).

Blood nourishing effect: Herbs like Danggui (Angelica sinensis)
and Shengdi (Rehmannia glutinosa).

Blood motility enhancement: Herbs like Danshen (Salvia mil-
tiorrhiza) and Rendongteng (Lonicera japonica).

TOPICAL TREATMENTS

Herbal bath: Soothing warm water infuses the power
of herbs through the largest organ in your body—your skin.

1. Place Chutaoye (Folium Broussonetiae, 250 g) and Cebaiye
   (Cacumen Platycladi, 250 g) in 1 ½ gallons of water
2. Boil for 20 minutes
3. Cool to proper temperature
4. Strain out the herb and add to bath water
5. Repeat twice or three times per week
6. The above formula is suitable for various patterns of skin erup-
   tions, but it is used with caution in the acute stage

Herbal ointment and paste: A blend of herbs as described
above in Herbal and Food Remedies, such as Shengdi, Danpi,
Xuansheng, and Danshen, warmed in cocoa butter, lanolin, or oils
are rubbed on the skin as an external psoriasis treatment.

EVERY BREATH YOU TAKE:
Respiratory Problems

Common respiratory complaints—cough, asthma, sore throat—are attributed to the TCM Organ of the Lung. Lung essentially is a "dispersing and descending" Organ that controls respiration and a number of other related functions, such as perspiration.

As with most other TCM diagnoses, when the Lung has a problem, it falls largely under two categories: Deficiency (internal Organ functional loss) or Excess (external pathogen invasion). Therapies and preventive measures differ according to the TCM syndrome and individual conditions, but there are some common and easy-to-follow measures that are suitable for most people:

SELF-MASSAGE: This massage works for most people with Lung deficiency and deficiencies of other related Organs, but especially well for children.

» To tonify the Spleen, stroke 100 times on the radial side of the thumb from the tip towards the wrist.

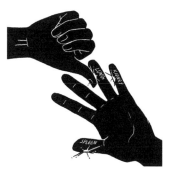

» To tonify the Lung, stroke 100 times on the radial side of the ring finger from the tip towards the palm.

» To tonify the Kidney, stroke 100 times on the radial side of the little finger from the tip towards the palm.

ENVIRONMENT:

Stay away from pathogens—maintain an appropriate indoor temperature and humidity.

Keep indoor air fresh—no smoking.

Maintain a good mood—especially for patients with Liver fire.

Make good food choices—avoid cold and raw food, excessive spices, sweets, fatty, fried and greasy food, and alcohol.

Provide nutrition support—supplements like vitamin C, zinc, and omega-3 fatty acid are recommended.

COUGH

Cough is a reflexive response to clear the lower airway when there's buildup of sputum or a foreign object (like food). It is one of the symptoms of upper respiratory infection— bronchitis, pleurisy, and pneumonia. TCM explains cough in its own way. As a "descending" Organ, Lung draws the inhaled air downward in its airway. That's how Lung Qi operates. When Lung Qi is upset, the airflow goes opposite with a brief, but strong, force.

Wind is the primary external pathogen that breaks the barrier of Protective Qi (see the chapter of Cold) to cause coughing. Internal pathogens include Dampness or Heat that are generated by unhealthy diets (see below), alcohol, or smoking. Dampness generates phlegm (a rattling cough with abundant sputum), and Heat dries up the lung (a bark cough).

In addition to the above coughs caused by external pathogens, Lung deficiencies may also result in a weak-sounding cough that mostly occurs in the late afternoon or evening.

HERBAL & FOOD REMEDIES

In TCM, different foods are used to treat a cough. One of the best foods for a cough is radish. Find recipes with this powerful ingredient, along with our calming Pork and Almond Soup recipe, in our recipes section. If you're prone to cough, avoid excessive spices, sweets, fats, fried and greasy food, and cold and raw food. Here are a few more of our favorite cough-suppressing recipes:

Steamed fresh pears:

1. Peel and cut open fresh pears and remove the core
2. Add some rock sugar
3. Steam until softened

Tofu nest: Good for clearing Heat and Dryness.

1. Create a bowl shape from 16 oz. of tofu
2. Add ½ cup each of brown and white sugar
3. Steam for 30 minutes

Nut tonic: Helps those with chronic cough with no symptoms of phlegm, shortness of breath, or dry throat.

1. Combine peanut (¼ cup) with ginkgo (2 Tbsp.), lily bulb (2 Tbsp.), and northern Shashen (Radix Glehniae, 2 Tbsp.)
2. Add a ½ tsp. of rock sugar
3. Stew to decoction and drink the juice once a day

ASTHMA

Asthma is principally characterized by a shortage of air into the lungs, to the point of breathing open-mouthed with raised shoulders and an inability to lie down. It is symptomatic of airway obstruction, hyper-responsiveness, and inflammation. Common cold is also a trigger for asthma, which explains why it often occurs in fall and winter seasons.

In TCM, Wind, an external pathogen, is the primary culprit in allergic asthma. Wind contracts, it comes and goes in bouts, and it causes spasm. The Wind referred to here may be compared to Western medicine allergens: dust, mites, pollen, and animal dander.

HERBAL & FOOD REMEDIES

In TCM, different foods are used to treat asthma. One of the best foods for asthma is duck. Find recipes with this powerful ingredient, along with our Duck Soup with Ginger recipe, in our recipes section. While there, look for these other favorite, asthma-focused recipes:

Honey ginger juice: Soothes asthma after a cold.

White radish pepper soup: Good for people who are depressed and have thick, excessive phlegm that is difficult to cough up.

Almond grain rice tea: Best for those with internal Organ deficiencies, poor appetite, and cough with white sputum.

Chrysanthemum-platycodon-snow pear soup: Invigorates Lung Qi, clears Heat and relieves cough. Ideal for those with cough, asthma, and yellow sputum.

BELLY BREATHING

1. Sit in a comfortable position
2. Place one hand just above your navel and your other hand on your chest
3. Breathe in deeply through your nose while staying relaxed, allowing your belly to expand, and feeling your hand rise as it rests on your stomach
4. Breathe out through pursed lips, similar to whistling
5. Repeat your inhale and exhale 10 times

SORE THROAT

The most common cause of a sore throat is a viral infection (pharyngitis), such as a common cold or the flu. Strep throat (streptococcal infection) is a less common type of sore throat caused by bacteria. Depending on the length of the ailment, the symptom may be classified as acute or chronic. Often, symptoms include a red and swollen laryngopharynx, dryness, and the feeling of a foreign object in the throat.

TCM calls it "Throat Impediment," Acute sore throat is mostly attributed to the Excess syndromes (related to Wind, Heat, and Dampness), whereas chronic sore throat is Excess accompanied by Lung deficiency. Regardless of the duration of the symptoms, both acute and chronic impediments lead to stagnation or obstruction of Qi and Blood, hence the pain.

SELF-MASSAGE
ZHAOHAI ACUPOINT MASSAGE:
This acupuncture point is located on the inner side of the foot, in the depression below the tip of the inner ankle. When you feel soreness, numbness, and swelling

during pressing, the effect of improving Lung Qi has been achieved. Mild soreness is sufficient. Press for 5-10 minutes. In order to enhance the effect of clearing the larynx and throat, you can also press the Taixi point (see page 214), alternatively, in a similar manner.

PINCH EARLOBE: Use your point finger and the thumb to pressure the bottom edge of the ear lobes for 1-2 minutes.

HERBAL & FOOD REMEDIES

In TCM, different foods are used to treat a sore throat. One the best foods to relieve sore throat symptoms is green tea. Look for this and other sore throat-nurturing tea recipes in our recipe section:

Honeysuckle tea: Expels pathogens in the respiratory tracts associated with sore throat.

Peppermint tea: Available in grocery stores in tea bags. Place in boiling water.

Snow pear and monk fruit tea: Good for those with Lung Yin Deficiency (characterized by dry cough or sticky sputum, dry mouth, and sometimes loss of voice).

ALLERGIC RHINITIS

Allergic rhinitis is due to an antigen-antibody reaction in the nasal cavity lining. Common symptoms include: sneezing, running nose, stuffy nose, itchy nose and eyes, watery eyes, frequent headache, etc. If the allergic response is only to pollen, it is called seasonal allergic rhinitis or hay fever. If the antigens are dust, animal dander, and fungal spores, it's called perennial allergic rhinitis.

In TCM, the root of allergic rhinitis is believed to be the Lung Qi deficiency or Kidney Yang deficiency. Both Organs have the function of "descending air." Nonetheless, the acute phase of the ailment often manifests as the invasion of Wind-Cold (clear mucus) or Wind-Heat (thick-yellow mucus, redness and swelling around the nose) in the Lung.

SELF-MASSAGE
NASAL MASSAGE:
Rub your hands back and forth until your palms are warm, then massage up and down along the sides of the nose with your middle fingers. Massage the top to the hairline and the bottom to the root of the nose and repeat 30 times. Do this three times a day.

HERBAL & FOOD REMEDIES
In TCM, different foods are used to treat the different phases allergic rhinitis. The following recipes treat the Wind-Cold type, Wind-Heat type, and Lung and Kidney Yang deficiency.

Japonica rice, chicken, ginger, and jujube porridge: For allergic rhinitis of Wind-Cold type.

Chrysanthemum and mulberry leaves porridge: Suitable for allergic rhinitis of Wind-Heat type.

Ginger and walnut soothing drink: For allergic rhinitis of Lung and Kidney Yang deficiency

Look for these and more in our recipe section.

THE KITCHEN SINK
Issues Along the Digestive Tract
Spleen and Stomach together are called the "the foundation of life after birth." A problem with this foundation may lead to all kinds of issues, for example: indigestion, heartburn, hemorrhoid, diarrhea, constipation, and abdominal pain. In the G.I. Woe chapter, we talked in length about these symptoms and how they are explained and treated by TCM.

The TCM Organ Stomach works in a Yin and Yang pair with Spleen. While Spleen governs food transportation and transformation, Stomach controls reception and digestion. The Spleen works like a "propeller", while the Stomach is compared to a "holder." You may recall one of the essential features of Qi is movement. The Spleen-Qi moves up and the Stomach-Qi moves down. Only when the ascent of Spleen-Qi and descent of Stomach-Qi work in sync will digestion and absorption be normal. When they are out of sync, you experience poor appetite, bloating, gastric reflux, heartburn, constipation, or hemorrhoids.

TCM treatment works to rebalance Yin and Yang. This includes readjusting the environment, foods, and lifestyle, and the Yin (Spleen) and Yang (Stomach) Organ. Here are some common tips for protecting your Spleen and Stomach:

- » **Choose the right foods:** Avoid excessive amounts of fatty, greasy, or spicy foods and cold drinks. These foods carry pathogens like Dampness, Heat, or Cold and upset Spleen and Stomach.
- » **Eat in moderation**: Gluttony is a top killer of Spleen and Stomach. Dampness slips in while the food backs up in the Stomach, and indigestion and bloating soon follow suit.
- » **Don't skip meals**: The functioning of Spleen and Stomach Qi depends on regular feeding. Starving yourself causes malnutrition, anemia, and weakness.
- » **Be careful of medications**: Long-term or excessive use of painkillers can damage the Qi and Blood of the Spleen and Stomach and cause discomfort, even bleeding in severe cases.
- » **Stay positive**: Emotional stress such as anxiety harms the Spleen and anger harms the Liver which, in turn, disrupts the running of Spleen and Stomach Qi (Liver Qi stagnation).
- » **Mindful chewing**: Chew thoroughly and swallow your food slowly for better digestion.
- » **Massaging the abdomen**: See chapter on GI Issues (page 117).

HEARTBURN

Heartburn is also called gastroesophageal reflux disease, or GERD. It happens when the muscle around the bottom of the esophagus cannot stop the acid in the stomach from swelling up. Symptoms often occur when you are under a high level of stress, after a big meal, and during sleep. They include belching and frequent burning in the chest. Taking antacids may relieve symptoms temporarily, but they are often reoccurring and lingering.

Abnormal flow of gastric fluid indicates a problem with Qi movement. The primary cause is Spleen and Stomach Qi deficiency (poor appetite, fatigue, loose stools, and cold intolerance), Stomach Yin deficiency (eating gives temporary relief, dry mouth and throat, dry stools or constipation is common), Phlegm Dampness (heaviness in the body, pear shaped and overweight, greasy skin, and musty body odor), and Liver Qi invading the Stomach (stress, hypochondriac, epigastric tenderness, fullness, or discomfort).

HERBAL & FOOD REMEDIES

In TCM, different foods are used to treat heartburn, and some foods are best to avoid. If you're prone to heartburn, stay away from coffee, alcohol, pepper, sweet treats, and fatty meals. Look for these powerful heartburn—reducing recipes in our recipe section:

Chinese yam lily porridge: Nourishes Stomach Yin and promotes body fluid. It works well for Spleen Qi deficiency.

Zhuru japonica rice porridge: Clears away Heat to soothe the Stomach.

Carrot rose and brown sugar water: Soothes the Liver and invigorates the Stomach. Best for those with Liver Qi invading the Stomach.

INDIGESTION

Approximately 20 percent of people globally have this condition. Unhealthy diets, too much alcohol, carbonated beverages, anxiety, certain antibiotics, and pain relievers may lead to early fullness during a meal. Common symptoms of indigestion include: uncomfortable fullness after a meal, bloating, poor appetite, belching, nausea, and vomiting.

In TCM, Spleen and Stomach are the Organs to blame for indigestion. Indigestion symptoms are among those of Spleen deficiency described frequently in this book. This deficiency may have congenital causes, but more often it's a result of unhealthy diet and overeating, eating too quickly, consuming cold drinks, and overindulging in fatty, greasy, or spicy foods that carry Dampness. Bad diets also cause indigestion by bringing Heat (or Fire) that injures Stomach Yin.

Another potential culprit in indigestion may be traced to Liver (the universal "dredger"). Liver Qi stagnation, a common problem associated with emotional stress, would understandably reveal itself through upsetting Spleen and Stomach Qi.

HERBAL & FOOD REMEDIES

In TCM, different foods are used to treat indigestion, and some foods are best to avoid. If you're prone to indigestion, eliminate fatty foods and overeating. Look for these powerful indigestion–reducing recipes in our recipe section:

Dried ginger and tangerine peel powder: Used to warm the Spleen to remove Dampness.

Orange peel drink: Power up Qi and invigorate Spleen

HEMORRHOIDS

It is noticeable if swollen blood vessels (varicose veins) appear on your arms or legs. But when your stool reveals surface blood or something protrudes from the anus, you become acutely aware the same is happening down below. Doctors call it hemorrhoids. Hemorrhoids are often caused by sitting and standing for long periods of time, carrying heavy loads for long distances, and pregnancy. The common symptoms include bright red bleeding seen on stool or toilet tissue, itching, uncomfortableness, or pain during bowel movements.

In TCM, hemorrhoids are attributed to local pathogens (Dryness, Heat, and Dampness) compounded by Spleen deficiency (if you recall, the function of the Spleen is ascending). Going by the most prominent symptoms, hemorrhoids are classified into three major syndromes: 1) Qi stagnation and Blood stasis—the prolapse of an intrarectal lump, even incarceration or thrombosis in the anal border, edema, pain, and tenderness; 2) Downward transmission of Dampness-Heat—local swelling, pain, and moistness; 3) Spleen-Qi deficiency and sinking—prolapse of anus and fatigue.

LEVATOR ANUS: (see page 105)

CHENGSHAN:

1. Locate the Chengshan acupoint at the center of the depression when the calf muscles contract
2. Lie on your back, bend your knees approximately 90-degrees
3. Place your right thumb on the right Chengshan, left thumb on the left Chengshan
4. Apply pressure perpendicularly, and press and knead both points for one minute
5. Repeat three sets twice per day

QIHAI:

1. Locate Qihai on the midline of the abdomen, two fingers' width (index and middle fingers) below the navel
2. Lie on your back, place left thumb on the Qihai, right thumb on top of the left thumb to increase strength
3. Apply pressure steady and per-pendicularly, hold for one minute
4. Meanwhile, contract the pelvic muscles and hold for 3-5 sec-onds, then relax
5. Repeat 3 sets twice per day

HERBAL THERAPY

Chinese Medicine treatment of hemorrhoids is often washing—a sitz bath. The commonly used herbal ingredients are Wubeizi (Galla Chinensis, 30 g), Kushen (Radix Sophorae Flavescentis, 20 g), Huangbai (Cortex

Phellodendri, 20 g), Shanzhizi (Fructus Gardeniae, 20 g), Mingfan (Alumen, 30 g).

1. Mix all the above-mentioned medicinal materials and put into a cloth bag
2. Place the bag in a pot. Add 12 cups water and boil for 15 minutes
3. Pour mixture, including the medicine bag, into the sitz tub
4. Take a bath that's the right temperature for you
5. Use once a day for 30 minutes

HERBAL & FOOD REMEDIES

In TCM, different foods are used to treat hemorrhoids, and some foods are best to avoid. If you're prone to hemorrhoids, stay away from spicy foods and overeating. Look for these powerful, symptom-reducing recipes in our recipe section:

Banana water spinach porridge: Clears away Heat and detoxification, moistens the intestines, and works as a laxative.

Sophora japonica soup: Cools Blood to stop bleeding and remove Heat.

Flower tea: Enhances Qi and Blood movement. Use herbs such as honeysuckle and chrysanthemum. Works well for those with Qi stagnation and Blood stasis.

LET'S KEEP THIS PRIVATE:
Issues Happening Below the Belt

From the TCM perspective, problems of the urinary and reproductive system often come down to Kidney and Bladder issues. Kidney is the Yin Organ that carries the function (Kidney Qi) through the substance Jing (see Chapter 7 on Low Libido). And bladder is the Yang Organ that interfaces with the exterior and serves as the conduit for urine transport. One prominent issue with Kidney is its tendency to lose Jing, hence the deficiency of Kidney Qi. This deficiency is not only seen in low libido, but a variety of other conditions: benign prostate hyperplasia (BPH), lower back pain, fading memory, hair loss, and osteoporosis. Many of these conditions come after a certain age—the older you get, the worse the problem becomes.

PROSTATIC ENLARGEMENT / HYPERPLASIA

By the age 60, half of males will have an enlarged prostate, a condition also known as benign prostatic hyperplasia, or BPH. By age 85, the number reaches 90 percent. BPH is characterized mainly by a frequent or urgent need to urinate, difficulty urinating, weak urine stream or a stream that stops and starts, dribbling of urine, and increased urination at night. When the prostate enlarges, it begins to block urine flow and causes annoying and embarrassing urination problems.

In TCM, this condition belongs to a disease category of "retention of urine." Besides the Kidney and Bladder, the Lung is also involved (recall the Lung is a "descending" Organ that not only controls the inhalation but also urination). Here are the accompanying symptoms:

> » **Kidney Yang deficiency**—pale complexion, short breath, lassitude, cold sensation in the limbs, aversion to cold, impotence.
>
> » **Lung-Qi failing to disperse**—pain in the penis, distending fullness in the lower abdomen, shortness of breath, excessive thirst, constipation.
>
> » **Damp Heat in the Bladder**—yellow, brown, and hot urine, itching and pain in the urethra, distending fullness or pain in the lower abdomen, may also be accompanied by hematuria, dry mouth, constipation.

MOVEMENT THERAPY

LEVATOR ANUS (as described in Low Libido chapter): Promotes local blood circulation.

1. Clamp the hips and thighs as you sit, lie, or stand

2. Lift the anus upwards while inhaling deeply (such as holding back urine or stool)
3. Hold your breath for 5–10 seconds and then exhale
4. Relax your whole body
5. Complete 20–30 reps, 2–3 times per day

HUIYIN POINT MASSAGE: The Huiyin (perineum) point is the meeting point of three important meridian: Du Mai, Ren Mai, and Chong Mai.

1. Lie on your back with your legs bent and apart
2. Use the middle finger to knead the perineum (between the anus and the scrotum) 50 times in a clockwise direction
3. Repeat the massage in a counterclockwise direction knead the perineum 50 times using your other middle finger.

HERBAL & FOOD REMEDIES

In TCM, different foods are used to treat an enlarged prostate. Look for these powerful prostate–loving recipes in our recipe section:

Winter melon (wax gourd) and rice soup: Clears away Heat and promotes urination.

Stewed duck with american ginseng: Nourishes Qi and Kidney Yin.

Cinnamon porridge: Warms and tonifies Kidney Yang while promoting Blood circulation and urination.

OVERACTIVE BLADDER

Overactive bladder causes an increase in urination and a sudden urge to urinate that may be difficult to control, as well as incontinence. It occurs because the muscles of the bladder start to contract involuntarily, even when the volume of urine in your bladder is low.

In TCM, this condition involves deficiencies of Yin Organs (Kidney, Spleen, and Lung) and the presence of pathogens (Damp-Heat) in the Yang Organ bladder. The following are the major differentiating syndromes:

» **Kidney-Yang deficiency**—prolonged urination, clear urine, urine incontinence, tiredness and coldness, sore waist and knees, weakness in both lower limbs.

» **Spleen-Lung-Qi deficiency**—fatigue, weakness, incontinence when coughing, crying, shortness of breath, reluctance to talk, poor appetite, loose stools, bloated feeling in the lower abdomen.

» **Damp Heat in the bladder**—hot and smelly urine, frequent urination, dripping, occasional incontinence, or astringent and painful urination indicates the invasion of Dampness and Heat. Dampness-Heat in the bladder can also cause urinary incontinence.

MOVEMENT THERAPY
ANUS FLOW EXERCISE:

1. While standing or sitting, contract the abdominal muscles
2. Exhale slowly through your mouth, while lifting your anus upwards
3. Close the anus tightly, contract your lower abdomen forcefully
4. Hold your breath and keep the anus lifted for 3–5 seconds
5. Relax your abdomen and anus slowly and relax your whole body
6. Repeat the above steps for 5-10 minutes

HERBAL & FOOD REMEDIES

In TCM, different foods are used to treat an overactive bladder. Look for these powerful bladder-loving recipes in our recipe section:

Chinese yam porridge: Warms the Spleen and Stomach, replenishes Qi, and restrains urination.

Soybean sprout soup: Clears away Heat and Dampness.

IMPOTENCE

Erectile dysfunction, or ED, also called "impotence," is the repeated inability to get or keep an erection firm enough for sexual activity. It can be caused by physical damage, diseases, lifestyle choices, surgery that can sever the nerves, medications, and psychological issues.

In TCM, an erection depends on Qi for the penis to become fully erect. The main Organs involved in the pathology of impotence are the Kidney, Liver, and Heart. The following are the major differentiating syndromes:

» **Kidney Yang deficiency**: Erection needs movement and action, a characteristic of Yang. Therefore, an erection needs Yang Qi deriving from Kidney-Yang (also called "the Fire of the Gate of Life"). Old age or excessive sexual activity deplete the Kidney-Jing and, along with it, Kidney-Yang, and may thereby cause impotence.

» **Heart Qi (or Blood) deficiency**: The penis needs the action of the Heart for erection in two ways. Firstly, Heart-Qi needs to descend to the penis to promote erection (Qi movement). Emotional stress, for instance, causes disturbance of the Spirit (mental activity) governed by the Heart, and as a result, erection fails. Secondly, the Heart governs Blood, what the penis needs to fill it to achieve an erection.

» **Liver Qi stagnation**: The Liver has an important influence on the penis, as the meridian of Liver runs through it. Liver also stores Blood that is necessary for erection to occur. For example, repressed anger and guilt may lead to Liver Qi stagnation and Blood stasis. The blood cannot reach the penis, which may cause erectile dysfunction.

SELF-MASSAGE
GROIN MASSAGE:

1. Use the thumb, index finger, and middle finger of both hands to massage the groin on both sides symmetrically from the outside to the root of the penis
2. Massage force should be gentle, comfortable, and painless

3. Repeat motion 50 times on each side

TESTICLE RUB:

1. Use the index and middle fingers of both hands to support the underside of the testicles on the same side
2. Press on it with your thumb and gently rub the testicles on both sides like a rosary
3. Rub each testicle 150–200 times

YONGQUAN MASSAGE (a common acupoint for strengthening the Kidney):

1. Massage the Yongquan acupoint in the middle of the right sole with the left hand 100 times
2. Massage the Yongquan acupoint in the middle of the left sole with the right hand 100 times
3. It's ideal to perform this massage treatment every night after a hot foot bath

LOWER BACK MASSAGE:

1. Place the palms of your hands on the same side of your waist near your back
2. Massage back and forth from top to bottom for about two minutes

LOWER ABDOMEN MASSAGE:

1. Before going to bed, place one hand on the lower abdomen under the navel
2. Place your other hand on the waist
3. Hold down the waist while slowly rubbing your lower abdomen with your hand, right to left, to feel warm at the abdomen
4. Repeat motion 100 times

LEVATOR ANUS: (see page 105)

HERBAL & FOOD REMEDIES

In TCM, different foods are used to treat impotence. Several foods have an effect on nourishing the Kidney and Essence, replenishing Qi, and invigorating Yang, such as: sea cucumber, oyster, eggs, grapes, lemon, black-bone chicken, soft-shelled turtle, lotus seeds, black sesame seeds, black beans, sheep kidney, walnut, chestnuts, pineapple, cherries, leeks, pepper, ginger, green onions, lychees, shrimp, beef, etc. One of the best foods for impotence is lamb. Find recipes with this powerful ingredient, including Lamb Soup with Ginger and Pepper, in our recipes section. While there, look for this other favorite impotence-ridding recipe:

> **Shrimp simmered lamb:** Invigorates the Kidney and Yang. Used
> for Kidney deficiency and impotence in the elderly.

FOR WOMEN ONLY:
Problems Associated with Female Systems

Female sex hormones—estrogen, progesterone, etc.—are at the core of female reproductive physiology. Gynecological problems—menstrual, menopausal, and oncologic issues, and even fertility—are all essentially hormonal disorders.

In TCM, given the reproductive process is governed by the Kidney, the activity of sex hormones (and any associated issues) could be conceivably attributed to Kidney's Qi.

But there's another MVP here. Female hormonal activity is a highly dynamic process. Hormones rise and fall on a monthly basis (the menstrual cycle) and fluctuate throughout life (adolescence to menopause). At the time of pregnancy, these hormones go on a roller coaster ride. Such a dynamic certainly would call for the safeguard of another TCM Organ, the Liver (the "dredger"). Recall how we described this most abstract Organ of TCM in Chapter 5. Whenever there's a dynamic process, be it Qi movement, Blood flow, inhalation, or the movement of food in the GI tract, Liver Qi is there to clear the runway. You've been familiarized with the high-frequency term Liver Qi stagnation, a syndrome of problems that appear mostly in high-intensity places. The same applies to women's issues.

PREMENSTRAL SYNDROME (PMS) & MENSTRUAL CRAMPS

Nearly 2 in 3 women experience PMS between ovulation and their period, a condition likely caused by hormonal changes during the menstrual cycle. Symptoms include: mental issues (moodiness, anxiety, depression), migraine, cravings, cramps, and water retention. They can last 2 or 3 days, or longer. Menstrual cramp refers to the pain in the lower abdomen and lower back before or during menstruation, accompanied by dizziness, soreness of the waist, nausea, cold sweat, and cold limbs in severe cases. As many as 40 to 50 percent of women suffer from menstrual pain, with about 10 percent of young women experiencing symptoms so severe they cannot participate in their normal activities during this period.

From the TCM point of view, menstrual cramps and PMS have similar etiology, only PMS displays wider spectrums of clinical symptoms. To go by the principle: "Where there is pain, there is obstruction," the primary problem here is Qi stagnation and Blood stasis. Further differentiation often reveals underlying pathologies, such as Liver Qi stagnation (breast tenderness, stomachache, blurred vision, insomnia, fatigue, depression), Liver and Kidney deficiency (lower back and knee ache, low vitality, dizziness, tinnitus), Cold invasion of the uterus (pain relieved by external warmth).

HERBAL & FOOD REMEDIES

According to TCM nutrition standard, a good diet for PMS and menstrual pain should include fresh vegetables, fruits, whole grains, legumes, nuts, seeds, and deep sea fish. Most importantly, all foods should be organically produced to guarantee the purity and quality of what we consume on daily basis. Because PMS is a hormone-related condition, many individuals get quick relief when they have improved nutrition. Look for our Lily, Lotus Seed, and Chinese Date Porridge recipe, along with these other powerful PMS-supporting tea and porridge recipes in our recipe section:

Ginger and scallion root tea: This hot beverage is a traditional Chinese remedy for Cold-caused menstrual cramps and stomach ache. It quickly relieves the pain and dissolves mild stagnation.

Rose tea: An aromatherapy effect relaxes the mind and improves mood, while relieving PMS symptoms and mild lower abdomen pain. **Lotus seed porridge:** Good for moving Qi and Blood, particularly effective for tonifying Kidney and calming the Spirit (mind). Made with lotus (30 g), ginger (10 g), Chinese date (10 g), and rice (80 g).

You can find other self-care remedies associated with easing PMS and menstrual cramps at the end of the next Endometriosis and Uterine Fibroid section.

ENDOMETRIOSIS AND UTERINE FIBROID

Both conditions are characterized by extra tissue growth within the reproductive system. In endometriosis, endometrial cells from the lining of the uterus migrate to locations where they are not normally seen—in the uterine myometrium and outside of the uterus or ovaries, or any other area of the pelvic cavity. It affects millions of child-bearing age women. Symptoms include painful periods (including lower back pain and abdominal cramping), painful intercourse, painful intestinal upset, frequent urination during menstruation, and infertility. Fibroids are the most common abnormal growth in the uterine muscle and connective tissue. They develop following the onset of menstruation, enlarge during pregnancy, and gradually shrink after menopause. Fibroids are benign tumors found in approximately 20 percent of childbearing age women. This condition causes menstrual cramps, excessive menstrual bleeding, and infertility.

TCM sees tumors primarily from the angle of "Qi stagnation and Blood stasis." Local accumulation of Qi or Blood would conceivably lead to unwanted growth. But the root of the problem comes from "hiccups" in a supposedly smooth process where Yin and Yang are perfectly balanced. This point of view seamlessly aligns with recent advances in Western medicine. The genesis of a tumor has been shown to lie in the balance of oncogenes (genes that stimulate cell growth) and tumor suppressor genes (genes that keep the growth in check).

In the case of endometriosis and uterine fibroid, the pathology of "Qi stagnation and Blood stasis" occurs in the uterus, resulting in different forms of tumor. Syndrome differentiation could also reveal Liver Qi stagnation, Cold invasion to the uterus, Liver, and Kidney deficiency, etc. It's interesting to see these pathologies bear similarity to PMS and menstrual pain. This allows quite different diseases in Western medicine to be viewed similarly with TCM. After all, these are all disorders of hormones with a high degree of dynamics.

SELF-CARE

QIGONG: A regular, moderate practice of 30 minutes each day can help improve circulation and mood.

1. Sit or lie down in a quiet room
2. Focus on the Guanyuan point four fingers' width under your navel
3. Breathe in, hold, then slowly breathe out
4. Repeat this inhale and exhale pattern, making sure each breath is deep and slow

HERBAL BATH: Take a warm bath with essential oils like lavender, rosemary, rose and juniper (TCM aromatherapy) to relieve abdominal pain, mental stress, and relax the body and mind.

HOT WATER FOOT SOAK: Many women with Kidney deficiency have cold feet and hands. Soaking the feet before going to bed at night can improve sleep, promote circulation, increase the blood flow to the pelvic Organs, and relieve pain. Meridians of the Liver and Kidneys pass through the uterus and down to the feet. Soaking your feet increases Liver and Kidney Qi, while also relaxing the body and enhancing mood.

Before sleep, soak both feet in hot water that's at least three inches over your ankles. Soak for 30–40 minutes, adding more hot water to keep the temperature very warm. The overall effect is the same as a hot bath.

HERBAL & FOOD REMEDIES

In TCM, different foods are used to treat endometriosis. Foods that are especially good for resolving Blood stasis and Qi stagnation include saffron, Danggui (Radix Angelica Simensis), goji berry, lemons, onion, carrot, apple and celery. Look for recipes with these powerful, pain-easing ingredients in our recipe section.

TCM HERBAL SUPPLEMENTS: Both endometriosis and fibroids are the result of long-period Blood stasis and Qi stagnation. Herbal supplements are needed as a part of daily nutrition. These remedies are available in Chinese herb stores:

Yunnanbaiyao—one of the most popular herbs in the Chinese family cabinet, this Florence Nightingale of powders can be used externally. It swiftly stops bleeding, disperses stagnation, relieves pain, and promotes rapid healing of wounds.

Danggui (Radix Angelica Sinensis) syrup—boasting angelica as its main ingredient, it may just be the best Blood tonic in Chinese pharmacopoeia. It nourishes Blood, promotes circulation, increases blood supply to the uterus, and enhances immunity. And better yet, it's good for long term consumption.

Eight Treasure Tea—a classic combination that nourishes Blood and tonifies Qi. An excellent herbal supplement for both Qi and Blood weakness.

MENOPAUSE

Menopause triggers a wide variety of symptoms including hot flashes, anxiety, depression, weight gain, water retention, and irritability. Hot flashes, in particular, manifest as a recurrent transient hot feeling often accompanied by flushing, sweating, and palpitation, followed by a chilling feeling as the flash passes. If not taken care, hot flashes may last more than a decade in some cases.

TCM attributes menopause problems to the Kidney and Liver Qi weakness, healed by tonifying the Liver and Kidney, rebalancing the Yin-Yang system through healthy lifestyle, optimizing nutrition, and proper exercise. In particular, TCM recognizes hot flashes as Kidney Yin deficiency, which throws the Yin-Yang balance to the dominance of Yang (hotness).

HERBAL & FOOD REMEDIES

In TCM, different foods are used to treat menopause. Look for our Beef Stew with Bitter Melon and Goji Berries and Papaya Fig Shake recipes, along with other powerful menopause–easing recipes in our recipe section and below:

Black bone chicken and ginseng goji berry soup: A tonic food, able to promote hormone balance, boost immunity, and supply the body with natural hormone. Great for menopausal individuals with Kidney and Liver deficiency. Black bone chicken is a delicious, nutritionally rich food. Good for Kidney Liver function weakness, and well known for its therapeutic effects for fatigue, malnutrition, strengthening of Organs, and treatment of all deficiencies.

Bitter melon stew: Prepare 2 bitter melons, 1 pound of port rib, garnished with 5 slices of ginger, 2 green onions, and 4 ¼ cups of water. Stew on low heat for one hour, and add black pepper at end. The recipe is good for replenishing Yin.

Mai gan dazao tang: In menopausal women, emotional conditions are very common. This decoction is able to relax the mind, relieve anxiety, and improve sleep. Because the formula consists of food ingredients, it's easy to cook and safe for long-term consumption. All this with three simple ingredients:

1. Combine 3 Tbsp. whole wheat, 12 g licorice, and 12 pieces Chinese date
2. Add 3 ⅓ cups water and ingredients in a pot
3. Bring to boil and simmer for 30 minutes
4. Enjoy!

TCM HERBAL SUPPLEMENTS: TCM offers simple herbal formulas to help menopause problems. As menopause is not pathological, these herbs are not drugs, only dietary supplements. Therefore, generally speaking, most of them are safe and effective for long-term use.

Chaste berry and Motherwort—Beneficial for hot flashes, anxiety, and depression.
Danggui (angelica) and Licorice—Blood and Qi tonic.

INFERTILITY

In general, a woman is suffering from infertility if she is unable to get pregnant (conceive) after more than a year of unprotected sex and her partner
has normal reproductive function. If the woman has never conceived, it is
primary infertility. If she has conceived previously, it is secondary infertility.

As the female reproductive process primarily depends on Kidney and
Liver in TCM, infertility is attributed to two syndromes with the following
symptoms: 1) Kidney Yang deficiency—always feels cold, the feet are especially cold at night, wakes up to urinate at least once or twice each night,
delayed menstruation with decreased and pale menses, occasional spotting
about a week before her period is due, BBT (basal body temperature)
stays low between the first day of her period and ovulation; 2) Liver Qi
Stagnation—long-term depression, stress, and feelings of dissatisfaction.

In recent years, TCM medicinals and acupuncture have been used in
treating various causes of infertility such as ovulation dysfunction, immune
dysfunction, polycystic ovary syndrome, and endometriosis. Researchers
have worked to combine the techniques of Traditional Chinese and
Western medicine in an attempt to promote follicle maturation and ovulation. Available data has shown
TCM can significantly increase the
chance of pregnancy while using
assisted reproductive technology (ART).

SELF-MASSAGE:

GROIN MASSAGE: To increases
blood flow to pelvic Organs, providing more nourishment to the uterus
and ovaries.

1. Put your fingertips on the large artery just beneath the crease in your groin between your thigh and lower abdomen (see fig).
2. Holding the pressure for 30-45 seconds
3. Release the pressure and let the blood flow normally
4. Repeat on the opposite side.
5. Perform three sets, twice a day up to ovulation or the day before embryo transfer, not beyond

Note: Do not perform this exercise if you are or might be pregnant, have high blood pressure, heart disease, circulatory problem, history of strokes, or detached retinas.

HERBAL & FOOD REMEDIES

In TCM, different foods are used to treat infertility. Your dietary choices can help increase Kidney Yang. Eat foods that tonify the Kidney system such as black beans, legumes, kelp, parsley, tofu, raspberries, walnuts, wild rice, spirulina, and wheat germ. Wheatgrass and barley grass also nourish Qi, Blood, and Essence. Look for recipes with these powerful, fertility-boosting ingredients in our recipe section.

REDUCE STIMULANT CONSUMPTION: Cut down on caffeine and other stimulant use, including alcohol and cigarettes. Nicotine is a serious killer—it ages the ovaries and makes the eggs resistant to fertilization. Second-hand smoke impairs fertility almost as much as smoking cigarettes yourself. Alcohol is particularly damaging if you fall into the damp or Liver Qi categories of disharmony.

BUT SERIOUSLY:
How TCM Can Assist with Major Conditions

After the advent of antibiotics, vaccines, and other medical advances, infectious diseases have largely been tamed by humans. Chronic diseases, on the contrary, have taken a sharp trend upward. In the U.S., cardiovascular diseases and cancer are the number one and two killers. More recently, debilitating ailments such as diabetes, obesity, and Alzheimer's disease are increasing at an explosive rate in the U.S. and other countries around the world. We must take these upticks seriously.

As Western medicine starts to grapple with these conditions, it's worthwhile to take a look at the ancient wisdom of TCM. As we stressed in *Yin Yang You*'s opening chapters, TCM's strength lies in preventive medicine, particularly chronic diseases. Its philosophical foundation is based on Yin-Yang balance, which allows TCM to look at the initial (or subclinical) stage with a much higher resolution than Western medicine. This is a time of swaying balance prior to the tipping point, a stage TCM names Organ deficiency.

As you read through this section, you'll find the key word "deficiency" appearing time and time again as we explain the nuances of these serious conditions. Following TCM measures to rectify deficiency should go a long way in curbing the epidemic number of people living with these conditions.

OBESITY

Since 1975, worldwide obesity has tripled. This condition is now officially recognized as a disease, and it's linked to cardiovascular disease, hypertension, diabetes, arthritis, and more. Obesity is not simply caused by overeating fatty foods and sweets—there's a complex interaction between one's culture, environment, lifestyle, genetic makeup, and psychology issues. Here's TCM's theory on obesity. The risk factors stress Spleen and cause Spleen Qi deficiency, which over time invites Dampness, a pathogen known to generate phlegm. In TCM, phlegm describes a variety of things that block a physiological process (or Qi movement). It includes sputum in the airway as well as atherosclerotic plaques in the arteries. In the case of obesity, phlegm refers to the buildup of fat tissue due to "clogged" metabolism.

BREATHING

As we have described in Chapter 5, breathing exercise is an important part of Qi Gong therapy. It improves somatic state by adjusting mental state. Daily breathing exercises can stimulate positive biofeedback between the endocrine and nervous systems to bring about a healthy state of relaxation, reduce stress hormone levels, enhance immune function, normalize brain rhythms and chemistry, and hence improve conditions such as anxiety, mood swings, and intense cravings. For the purpose of weight loss, the following three breathing methods are most helpful.

LONG BREATHING: Breathing method with full, deep, long inhalations and exhalations. Breathing naturally uses only about 75 percent of lung capacity, whereas long breathing works with the lungs' full capacity to increase the amount of oxygen absorbed. It is practiced sitting still, and works like a tonic to complement energy.

BELLY BREATHING:

1. Sit in a comfortable position
2. Place one hand just above your navel and your other hand on your chest
3. Breathe in deeply through your nose while staying relaxed, allowing your belly to expand, and feeling your hand rise as it rests on your stomach
4. Breathe out through pursed lips, similar to whistling
5. Repeat your inhale and exhale 10 times

REVERSE ABDOMINAL BREATHING: Internal abdominal pressure is greatly increased with this breath to enhance diaphragmatic massage of the vital Organs, giving an extra boost to Blood and Energy circulation and driving Qi into the marrow and up to the brain. This breathing technique is relaxing. And abdominal muscle movement can greatly reduce the feeling of hunger.

1. Lie in a comfortable position with your whole body relaxed
2. Breathe normally
3. As you inhale, instead of letting your abdomen expand outwards, contract your abdominal muscles to draw the abdominal wall inwards

4. On exhale, relax the muscles and let the abdomen expand outwards as the diaphragm rises

HERBAL & FOOD REMEDIES

The keys to achieving weight loss with foods are the same TCM principles as bodily balance and harmony—Yin and Yang, the "Force of Five," and obey the law of nature.

In TCM, different foods are used to treat obesity. The following ingredients and recipes for food and soup can help. Look for these recipes and others with the same powerful obesity–busting ingredients in our recipe section:

Plantain: A weight loss powerhouse to reduce water retention and absorption of fats.

Fennel seed: Improves digestion and enhances Yang Qi.

Murdock / Dandelion: Clears Liver fire and toxins.

Kelp / Seaweed: Treats a sluggish thyroid gland.

Mung bean and rice porridge: Ideal for balancing the body and mind, mung bean is considered one the most valuable foods for its ability to purge toxins from the body to help reach weight-loss goals.

Pearl barley and brown rice porridge: Recommended for individuals with a weak Spleen.

Tomato and vegetable soup: Good for people with blood sugar imbalance. Eat as much as you like for 5–7 days to reduce cravings and easily lose significant weight in a few weeks.

Barley water: Barley is highly nutritious, good for digestion, decongests the chest and expels Dampness.

Aduki bean porrige: Aduki bean is known for water retention and detoxification benefits.

DIABETES

Diabetes mellitus (DM) is a group of metabolic disorders characterized by abnormal blood glucose elevations. Roughly 1 in 10 Americans (34.2 million) have diabetes. Approximately 1 in 3 American adults (88 million)

have prediabetes. Diabetes happens when either the pancreas doesn't produce enough insulin (Type I diabetes) or the body's cells don't respond properly to insulin produced (Type II diabetes). It can lead to excess sugar in your blood with subsequent serious health problems.

In TCM, diabetes, particularly at its early stage, is attributed to Yin deficiency. Yin deficiency is characterized by loss of fluid due to polyuria (one of the major symptoms of diabetes) and is often associated with the presence of pathogen Fire (or Heat). Further differentiation of patients is usually made by the following syndromes: Fluid consumption due to Lung Heat (excessive thirst and thirst right after drinking water), Excessive Fire in the stomach (excessive hunger, emaciation, and heartburn), and Deficiency of Kidney Yin (profuse urination, cloudy urine, weakness and soreness in the loins and limbs, tinnitus).

HERBAL & FOOD REMEDIES

In TCM, different foods are used to treat diabetes. Look for these recipes and others with the same powerful diabetes–busting ingredients in our recipe section:

White fungus and black fungus soup: Clears away Heat to moisten Lung and nourish Kidney and Yin.

Goji and egg crepes: Nourishes the Kidney and Yin while it benefits Essence and improves eyesight.

Ginseng and asparagus congee: Nourishes Kidney Yin and replenishes Qi.

Grilled tofu: Replenishes the Spleen and Stomach, clears the Heat, and expels the pathogens.

CORONARY HEART DISEASE AND ATHEROSCLEROSIS

Coronary heart disease is one of the biggest killers in the U.S., accounting for more than 370,000 deaths every year. The cause is clear—blood flow to the heart is blocked in the coronary arteries by plaque. Plaque buildup not only brings on a heart attack (cardio-muscular infarction), but also chest pain (angina), and irregular heartbeat (cardiac arrhythmia), depending on the degree to which the artery is blocked.

TCM calls a heart attack correctly, and intelligently, "chest painful blockade." The "blockade" here refers to the running of Qi and Blood in the chest due to various reasons, such as Phlegm and Cold. Although TCM doesn't see the illness anatomically, hence no mention of atherosclerosis and coronary blockage, the ancient wisdom is quite telling here.

Syndrome differentiation helps TCM to pinpoint the specific culprit that causes the blockage. A distending pain indicates stagnation of Qi. If accompanied by a feeling of oppression or tightness of the chest, it also indicates the presence of phlegm. Burning pain denotes Heat (usually Phlegm-Heat). A very severe pain indicates retention of Cold in the blood vessels.

Now how does TCM analyze atherosclerosis, the chronic stage that leads up to an acute heart event? Here's where the deficiency comes in. First is Spleen deficiency due to unhealthy diets, which generates Dampness and subsequently phlegm. In addition, deficiency of Liver (an all-important "dredger" Organ) explains the stagnation of Qi.

SELF-MASSAGE: Massage the following points twice a day for five minutes. Both sides can be performed alternately:

PRESSURE POINT	BENEFIT	LOCATION	LOCATE IT
Neiguan:	Core acupoint for Chinese medicine to treat heart diseases since ancient China—almost all symptoms related to heart abnormalities can be addressed with this acupoint	Located about four fingers' width above the horizontal line of your wrists and between the two outer tendons	

Zusanli:	Help regulate the pulse; apply pressure when the pulse is irregular	This acupoint is one fingers' width next to the tibia and the four fingers' width below the connection of the two eyes (protrusions) of the outer knee	
Fenglong:	This point is important to open the chest and improve the circulation of Blood	Located 8 fingers' width above the outer ankle and 2 fingers' width from the edge of tibia	

HERBAL AND FOOD THERAPY:

1. Many traditional Chinese herbs have the effect of moving the Qi and Blood, such as Danshen (Radix Salviae Miltiorrhizae), Chuanxiong (Rhizoma Ligustici), Danggui (Radix Angelica Sinensis).

2. Removing the Dampness is achieved by strengthening the function of Spleen through herbs like ginseng, Astragulus, and Dangshen (Codonopsis pilosula) and through foods like Chinese yam, raw ginger, and Fuling (Poria Cocos Wolf). Keep unhealthy, Spleen-damaging dietary behavior (such as fats and sugar) at bay.

3. Eat sufficient amounts of fruits (such as strawberries, pineap-ples, oranges, red grapes), nuts (almonds, walnuts, sunflower seeds), fiber-rich vegetables (shiitake mushrooms and aspar-agus), and fish.

HYPERTENSION

In ancient Chinese Medicine, there is no disease called "hypertension," because there were no instruments to measure blood pressure at that time. Contemporary Chinese medicine started to analyze hypertension patients with its own unique "processor" (Syndrome Differentiation) and shed light to the major patterns with which the TCM Organs are impacted:

» **Liver-Fire flair:** Due to Liver Qi stagnation. Symptoms include red face and eyes, thirst, trouble sleeping, constipation, dark-yellow urine.

» **Rising of Liver Yang:** Due to Deficiency of Liver- and Kidney-Yin. Symptoms include lower backache, poor memory, tinnitus, dry throat, dry eyes.

» **Blood stasis:** Symptoms include epistaxis, chest pain, numbness of limbs.

SELF-MASSAGE:
QUCHI POINT:

1. Find the Quchi point by bending the elbow 90 degrees. The end point of the horizontal skin line on the outside of the elbow is Quchi

2. Bend the left arm slightly, press and knead the Quchi point on the left arm with the palm of the right hand 100 times

3. Switch left and right and repeat the above action

HEGU POINT:

1. Place half of the right thumb over the webbing between the thumb and point finger of the left hand, with the thumb's traverse skin line on the webbing's edge.

2. Knead the Hegu acupoint in a rotating manner with the thumb of the right hand for 2–3 minutes, feeling soreness each time

3. Switch the left and right hands and repeat above action

TAICHONG POINT:

1. Find Taichong point located about 1.5 cm above the space between the big toe and the second toe on both feet

2. Press this acupuncture point with the pad of your thumb for 5–8 minutes to feel soreness

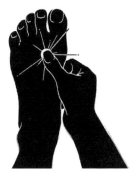

HERBAL & FOOD REMEDIES

A high-sodium diet raises blood pressure and potassium can promote the excretion of more sodium from the kidneys. High potassium foods like spinach, eggplant, potato, celery banana, fruits, nuts, and sweet potato help to lower blood pressure. And iodine-containing foods such as seaweed, jellyfish, and dried shrimp can reduce the deposition of cholesterol on the arterial wall. When it comes to foods to avoid, people with diabetes should not use rock sugar. Instead, simply use goji berries and cassia seed to make tea. Look for recipes with all these powerful, hypertension-lowering ingredients, including those mentioned below, in our recipe section.

Cassia seed / Goji berry: Both are known for their help to put out Liver Fire. Goji berry is also a tonifying agent that helps with Liver, Kidney, and Spleen deficiencies.

Kelp: A hypertension superfood—nourishing both Blood and Lung as it lowers blood pressure.

DEMENTIA / ALZHEIMER'S DISEASE (AD)

Fifty million people worldwide suffer from Alzheimer's disease and other kinds of dementia. AD, in particular, is growing at an alarming rate in recent years. It's a debilitating condition where, over time, patients lose their memory and cognitive abilities. Although AD attacks mainly older people, it is not necessarily an inevitable consequence of aging.

In TCM, the brain is considered "the ocean of marrow" and the Kidney stores Essence to generate marrow. Dementia is therefore believed to be a result of Kidney Qi deficiency. The tendency for a diagnosis to happen at an older age is explained by the loss of Kidney Essence over a lifetime. As a matter of fact, poor memory is one of the characteristic signs in the diagnosis of Kidney deficiency.

In the 21st century, renowned TCM professor Wang Yongyan from Beijing University of Chinese Medicine put forward a novel theory on AD. Dr. Yongyan believes that internally generated toxins damaging Brain and marrow is an important mechanism to explain the pathology of the disease in the industrial era. This theory mirrors oxidative damage in Western medicine and explains the rapid growth of AD in recent decades, particularly in the younger population.

SELF-MASSAGE

COMPLETE HEAD MASSAGE: Massaging the whole head is a good way to promote memory and prevent brain degradation.

1. Heat up both hands by quickly rubbing your palms together (Mr. Miyagi style)
2. Gently massage your whole head, starting by pressing down at the top
3. Move down to massage both sides
4. Move forward to massage your forehead, eyes, cheeks, and jaw
5. Move to the back of your head and end at the base of your skull
6. Massage for 5 to 10 minutes, two or three times daily

COMB HEAD MASSAGE: An alternative method to the complete head massage above, this form of massage is a direct way to stimulate head circulation, improve sleep quality, and also reverse brain degeneration.

1. Use a wooden comb, instead of your fingers, to stimulate the scalp
2. Massage scalp with comb at least 300 times, twice per day

MASSAGE TAIXI: Good for reinforcing the Kidney.

1. Find Taixi point located between the inner ankle and the Achilles tendon
2. Apply gentle pressure, gradually increase strength
3. Hold for a few minutes, 2–3 times per day

YONGQUAN: Take this simple step to increase Kidney Qi and improve the brain function.

1. Find Yongquan point located in the center of the bottom of your feet, a third of the way into your sole from your toes
2. Use finger joint to press it for two minutes, twice daily

MOVEMENT THERAPY

Regular, daily exercise of the slow, soft, rhythmic variety keeps circulation active and expels toxins and waste from the body. Deep breathing acts as a second heart to promote blood supply to the brain. Because the brain is the most sophisticated organ in your body, it demands a lot of nutrition. Together, meditation and breathing exercise remain the most effective, convenient methods for promoting brain vitality and preventing its degeneration.

HERBAL & FOOD REMEDIES

In TCM, a variety of different foods are used to treat Alzheimer's disease and dementia. Eating any type of fish is a wonderful way to feed your brain. Find recipes with this powerful ingredient, along with these favorite brain-loving recipes in our recipe section:

Chinese yam, goji berry and chicken soup: Chinese yam is tonic to Spleen and Kidney and goji berry is a tonic for the Liver and Kidney. Both nourish the brain and replenish Qi and blood.

Pollen and honey tea—Full of natural ingredients for healing and preventing diseases, while providing potent sources of essential fatty acids, amino acids, and trace elements.

Ginseng Sanqi tea—This herbal elixir tonifies energy, unblocks blood stasis, and is helpful for AD and vascular dementia sufferers.

RECIPES

SLEEP:
Longan, Lotus Seed, and Lily Bulb Soup

PREP TIME: 15 minutes + soaking time
COOK TIME: 40 minutes
SERVES: 2

2 Tbsp dried longans
⅓ cup dried lotus seed
½ cup dried lily bulbs
1 Tbsp rock sugar or coconut sugar
1 Tbsp dried osmanthus flowers

Place the longans and lotus seed in a small bowl and fill with water to cover. Soak for two to four hours at room temperature. Once softened, drain and rinse in a fine-mesh sieve. Split the lotus seeds in half and remove any dark germ in the center that could be bitter.

Add longans and lotus seed to a medium saucepan with the lily bulbs, rock sugar, osmanthus, and five cups water. Bring to a boil, then reduce to a simmer. Allow to simmer for 30 minutes or until ingredients are tender. Serve.

JOINT PAIN:
Coix Seed and Aduki Bean Congee

PREP TIME: 15 minutes + soaking overnight
COOK TIME: 35 minutes to 1 hour
SERVES: 4

⅓ cup Coix seed (Chinese pearl barley)
½ cup dried aduki beans or dried red kidney beans
3 Tbsp dried longans
⅓ cup rock sugar or coconut sugar
½ cup short grain white rice, rinsed (optional)

In a large bowl add the Coix seed and red bean and fill with water to cover by a couple of inches. Allow the mixture to soak for four hours up to overnight.

For the Pressure Cooker:
Drain the Coix seed mixture, rinse, and add to the bowl of an electric pressure cooker. Add the longans, five cups water, sugar, and rice (if using). Secure the lid and set to high pressure for 35 minutes. Allow to naturally release for 10 minutes, then quick release and remove the lid. Stir to combine and serve.

For the Stovetop:
Drain the Coix seed mixture, rinse, and add to a large pot. Add the longans, 6 ½ cups water, sugar, and rice (if using). Bring to a boil, then reduce to a simmer. Partially cover and allow to simmer for one hour until the beans and Coix seed are very tender. Be sure to stir frequently so the mixture doesn't stick to the bottom of the pot.

HEADACHE:
Astragulus Congee with Lotus Seeds and Dates

PREP TIME: 10 minutes + soaking time
COOK TIME: 1 hour
SERVES: 4

½ cup dried lotus seeds
½ cup + 2 Tbsp dried astragulus root
½ cup Chinese dates (about 12 dates)
½ cup short grain white rice, rinsed

Place the lotus seed in a medium bowl and cover with water. Allow to soak for four hours up to overnight.

Combine the astragulus and 2 ½ cups water in a medium pot and bring to a simmer. Cover and allow to simmer over low heat for 30 minutes. Strain through a fine mesh sieve, discarding the astragulus and keeping the tea. This should yield about 3/4 cup of tea.

After soaking the lotus seed, drain, and split the seeds in half and remove any green/brownish germ in the center. This is bitter, so remove and discard.

For the Pressure Cooker:
Add the astragulus tea to the bowl of an electric pressure cooker. Add the lotus seed, dates, rice, and 3 ¼ cups water (4 cups liquid total). Secure the lid and cook on high pressure for 30 minutes. Allow the pressure cooker to naturally release for 10 minutes, then quick release and stir. The rice should be broken down and very tender.

For the Stovetop:

Add the astragulus tea to a medium pot. Add the lotus seed, dates, rice, and 4 cups water (4 ¾ cups liquid total). Bring to a boil, then reduce to a simmer. Allow to simmer for 40 to 50 minutes partially covered until thickened and rice is very tender. Stir consistently toward the end of cooking to prevent the rice from sticking to the bottom of the pot, adding additional water as necessary.

ANTI-WRINKLE:
Astralagus Congee with Coix Seed, Mung Bean & Lotus Seed

PREP TIME: 5 minutes + soaking time
COOK TIME: 1 hour 40 minutes
SERVES: 4

⅓ cup Coix seed (Chinese pearl barley)
½ cup dried lotus seed
¼ cup dried mung beans
2 ¾ cup dried astragulus root
½ cup Chinese dates (about 12 dates)
½ cup short grain white rice, rinsed
1 Tbsp crushed rock sugar or coconut sugar, to garnish (optional)

In a large bowl add the Coix seeds, lotus seeds, and mung beans. Cover with water and allow to soak for at least four hours up to overnight.

Once softened, drain, and split the lotus seeds in half and remove any dark germ in the center that could be bitter.

In a medium saucepan add the astragulus and 4 ½ cups of water and bring to a boil. Cover and reduce to a simmer over low heat for 40 to 50 minutes. Strain the tea through a fine-mesh sieve, discarding the astralagus and set aside. This should yield about 1 ½ cups of tea.

For the Pressure Cooker:
Rinse the Coix seed mixture and add to an electric pressure cooker along with the Chinese dates, rice, 1 ½ cups of astragulus tea, and 4 ½ cups water (6 cups of liquid total). Seal the lid and cook for 30 minutes on high pressure. Allow to naturally release for 10 minutes, then quick release and stir to combine. The rice should break down, and seeds and beans should be tender. Serve with rock sugar, if desired.

For the Stovetop:

Rinse the Coix seed mixture and add to a large pot along with the Chinese dates, rice, 1 ½ cups of astragulus tea, and 6 ½ cups water (8 cups of liquid total). Bring to a boil, then reduce to a simmer over low heat.

Allow to simmer partially covered for 40 to 50 minutes until tender and thickened. Stir consistently during the last 15 minutes of cooking to avoid the rice sticking to the bottom of the pot. The rice should break down, and the seeds and beans should be tender. Serve with rock sugar, if desired.

COUGH:
Pork and Almond Soup

PREP TIME: 10 minutes
COOK TIME: 25 minutes
SERVES: 2

1 Tbsp canola oil
5 oz. pork butt, fat trimmed and cut into small cubes
2 cups chicken stock or water
½ tsp sea salt
½ cup Daikon radish, peeled and cubed
⅓ cup almond milk, unsweetened

Heat a medium saucepan over medium-high heat with oil. Add the pork butt and allow to cook until browned on all sides, 3 to 4 minutes. Remove the pork to a plate and wipe out the saucepan.

Add the chicken stock, salt, radish, and pork and bring to a simmer. Allow to simmer for 15 minutes until flavors have melded. Remove from the heat and stir in the almond milk right before serving.

ASTHMA:
Duck Soup with Ginger

PREP TIME: 15 minutes
COOK TIME: 2 hours
SERVES: 4

1 grapefruit
1 (4- to 5-pound) duck, giblets removed
⅓ cup walnuts
1 Tbsp sea salt
¼ cup Shaoxing cooking wine
½ cup sliced fresh ginger
2 star anise
2 to 3 fresh or dried bay leaves
Butcher's twine

Peel the grapefruit and leave the meat. Remove the internal organs of the duck and wash. Place the grapefruit slices and walnuts into the belly of the duck. Tie the legs of the duck together with butcher's twine.

Place the duck in a large pot and add water to completely cover by an inch or two. Add the salt, wine, ginger, star anise, and bay leaves. Bring to a boil, then reduce to a simmer over medium-low heat. Simmer partially covered for 1 hour 30 minutes, flipping the duck over every 30 minutes. When finished, the duck should be very tender, the meat on the wings almost falling off the bone.

Remove the duck from the soup and allow to cool to room temperature. Shred the duck meat, discarding the skin and bones.

Skim most of the fat from the top of the soup and place into a heat resistant bowl to cool. Discard the fat once cooled. Sip the broth with a little of the pulled duck meat in each bowl, if desired. Reserve the remaining duck meat for another use.

TIP: To easily skim the fat off the top of the stock, allow the stock to cool until warm. Place in heat resistant containers and chill in the refrigerator overnight. The fat will rise to the top. Skim the fat off and discard. Reheat the stock.

SORE THROAT:
Soothing Green Tea

PREP TIME: 5 minutes
COOK TIME: 15 minutes
SERVES: 1

2 Tbsp green tea
2 cups water
1 large pasteurized organic egg, separated
2 tsp crushed rock sugar or coconut sugar

Place the green tea into a tea ball or tea bag. In a small saucepan, bring water to a boil. Once boiling, turn off the heat, add the tea, cover the pot and allow to steep for 10 minutes. After steeping has finished, remove the tea ball or discard the tea bag.

Meanwhile, place the egg white in a medium bowl, reserving the yolk for another use. Add the rock sugar to the white and whisk until frothy (you can use chopsticks to do this as well). Pour the hot tea into the foamy egg white. Place the mixture in a mug and drink before sleeping.

Simplified version:
Whisk the egg white and rock sugar together until foamy. Swallow whenever the throat is uncomfortable. This mixture can be saved in the refrigerator for up to three hours.

BLADDER:
Leek and Walnut Porridge

PREP TIME: 5 minutes
COOK TIME: 20 minutes
SERVES: 1

¼ cup glutinous short grain rice, rinsed
¼ cup dried or fresh leeks (if using fresh, white and light-green parts only)
2 Tbsp walnuts
1 tsp sea salt, to taste

Place the leeks and walnuts into the bowl of a mini food processor and pulse until ground (if you don't have a mini food processor, just chop into small pieces). Set aside.

Drain the rice in a fine mesh sieve and rinse again. Add the rice, 1½ to 1¾ cups water, and salt to a medium saucepan and bring to a boil over high heat. Reduce to a simmer, and allow to cook for 10 to 15 minutes until rice is cooked through and mixture has thickened. Stir in the leek and walnut mixture. Eat on an empty stomach first thing in the morning.

IMPOTENCE:
Lamb Soup with Ginger and Pepper

PREP TIME: 10 minutes
COOK TIME: 30 minutes
SERVES: 1 to 2

1 Tbsp vegetable oil
⅓ cup (2.6 oz.) lamb, cut into small cubes
2 Tbsp russet potatoes, peeled and diced
3 Tbsp diced carrots, peeled and diced
5 Tbsp soy sauce
1 Tbsp Shaoxing cooking wine
1½ tsp crushed rock sugar or coconut sugar
2 Tbsp scallions, chopped
2 slices fresh ginger
1 tsp aniseed
1 tsp freshly ground black pepper

Using a wok or medium heavy-bottomed pot, add the vegetable oil and heat over high heat until almost smoking. Add the lamb and allow to cook for about three minutes, until browned. Remove the lamb to a plate and add the potatoes and carrots.

Allow the potatoes and carrots to fry until golden brown, three to four minutes. Then remove to the plate with the lamb. Carefully pour the hot cooking oil from the wok into a heat-resistant bowl and allow to cool.

Return the wok to the stove over low heat and add the lamb. Cover with four cups water and add the soy sauce, wine, sugar, scallions, ginger, aniseed, and pepper. Bring to a simmer and allow to simmer for 15 minutes or until the lamb is cooked through. During the last five minutes of cooking, add the potatoes and carrots and simmer for an additional five minutes. Serve.

PMS:
Lily, Lotus Seed, and Chinese Date Porridge

PREP TIME: 5 minutes + soaking time
COOK TIME: 1 hour 10 minutes
SERVES: 1

¼ *cup brown rice*
⅓ *cup dried lotus seed*
½ *cup dried lily bulb*
⅓ *cup Chinese dates (7 dates total)*

Place the brown rice and lotus seeds in a medium bowl and cover with water by a couple of inches. Allow to soak for one hour, then drain and rinse in a fine-mesh sieve. Split the lotus seeds in half and remove any dark seed germ in the center (this can be bitter).

Place the rice and lotus seeds, lily bulb, and dates into a medium saucepan. Add 4 ½ cups water. Bring to a boil, then reduce to a simmer. Allow to simmer for about an hour, until thickened and all ingredients are tender. Add additional water if necessary.

MENOPAUSE:
Beef Stew with Bitter Melon and Goji Berries

PREP TIME: 15 minutes
COOK TIME: 1 hour 30 minutes
SERVES: 4 to 6

2 Tbsp vegetable oil
2 tsp toasted sesame oil, plus additional to taste
2 lbs beef or lamb, fat trimmed and cut into 1-inch pieces
½ cup fresh ginger, thinly sliced
1 (1 lb) bitter melon, seeds removed and thinly sliced into half-moons, or baby
bok choy, thinly sliced
½ cup goji berry
Sea salt and freshly ground black pepper, to taste

Heat a wok or large cast iron skillet over medium-high heat with oil. Season the meat with salt and pepper. Add the meat and allow to cook until browned, about five to seven minutes. Remove to a large pot.

Add the ginger to the pot as well as seven to eight cups water. Bring to a boil, then reduce to a simmer over low heat. Cover the pot and allow to cook for one hour, adding more water as necessary.

Add the melon and goji berry and simmer another 15 minutes. Season with sea salt, pepper, and a couple of drops of sesame oil to taste.

TIP: If you want to remove some of the bitterness of the bitter melon, there are two methods. The first is to salt the sliced melon and allow it to sit at room temperature for one hour, then rinse. The second method is to blanch the melon in boiling water for three to four minutes, then immediately rinse under cold water before adding to the soup.

MENOPAUSE:
Papaya Fig Shake

PREP TIME: 15 minutes
SERVES: 2 to 3

3 dried figs
½ (3.5 pound) large papaya (4 cups), skin peeled and seeds removed, cut into 1-inch pieces
1 Tbsp honey
1 oz/ organic soy protein powder
2 cups filtered water

Soak the dried figs in hot water to soften for 10 minutes. Drain.

To the carafe of a blender add the papaya, figs, honey, protein powder, and water. Blend until very smooth. Serve.

OBESITY:
Aduki Bea, Brown Rice, & Oat Porridge with Peanuts & Sesame

PREP TIME: 5 minutes + soaking overnight
COOK TIME: 1 hour 10 minutes
SERVES: 1 to 2

¼ cup dried aduki bean
3 Tbsp brown rice
¼ cup old fashioned rolled oats
1 Tbsp dried lotus seeds
1 Tbsp roasted unsalted peanuts, plus additional to garnish
1 Tbsp black sesame seeds, plus additional to garnish
2 slices dried Chinese yam

In a large bowl combine the aduki beans, rice, and oats. Cover with water by a couple of inches and allow to soak overnight at room temperature.

Place the lotus seed in a separate small bowl and cover with water. Allow to soak for four hours. Once softened, split the seeds and discard any brown germ found inside.

Drain and rinse the bean mixture and lotus seeds, and place in a medium pot with the peanuts, sesame seeds, and yam. Add five cups water, then bring to a boil over high heat. Once boiling, reduce to a simmer over low heat and allow to cook for 40 to 50 minutes. During the last 20 minutes of cooking, stir consistently to avoid sticking to the bottom of the pot. Serve garnished with additional peanuts and sesame seeds.

DIABETES:
Tofu and Shiitake Mushroom Soup

PREP TIME: 10 minutes
COOK TIME: 25 minutes
SERVES: 4

1 (14 oz.) container soft tofu, drained
1 (3.5 oz.) container shiitake mushrooms, stemmed and quartered
2 tsp sea salt
Soy sauce, to serve
Toasted sesame oil, to serve
Scallions, thinly sliced to garnish (optional)

Pat the tofu dry and cut into ½-inch cubes. Place in a large pot with the shiitake mushrooms. Cover with eight cups of water, and season with salt. Bring to a boil over medium heat, then reduce to a simmer and allow to cook for 15 minutes.

Season to taste with soy sauce and sesame oil. Serve garnished with scallions.

BRAIN:
Tuna with Coconut Cream and Veggies

PREP TIME: 15 minutes
COOK TIME: 20 minutes
SERVES: 4

1 lb fresh sushi-grade tuna or salmon fillet, skin removed, cut into 1-inch cubes
2 lemons, juiced
½ tsp sea salt, plus additional to taste
1 medium white onion, thinly sliced
1 carrot, peeled and thinly sliced into matchsticks
1 green bell pepper, stemmed, seeded, and thinly sliced
2/3 cup coconut cream, well-stirred
2 Tbsp chopped roasted and salted peanuts, to garnish
1 Tbsp toasted sesame seeds, to garnish

Place the fish into a large glass bowl and add the lemon juice and salt. Toss to evenly coat the fish, then cover and allow to marinate at room temperature for 20 minutes.

Drain off the excess marinade of the fish and discard. Add the onion, carrot, and bell pepper to the fish and pour over the coconut cream. Toss to evenly combine and serve garnished with peanuts and sesame seeds. Season with additional salt, as desired.

MORE RECIPES

Gegeng-Ciwujia Congee

1. Prepare Gegeng (50 g) ¼ cup, rice or barley (50 g) ¼ cup, and Ciwujia (15 g)
2. Clean and mince the GeGeng
3. Boil Ciwujia, filter, and discard the raw herb
4. Place all materials (including the rice or barley) in a pot, add water, and heat to boiling
5. Put on low heat until rice or barley forms congee
6. Add a bit rock sugar

Red Bean & Sponge Gourd Vein Soup

1. Prepare red bean (30 g), sponge guard vein (9 g), Danggui (9 g), Chinese Clematis (dried root and stem, 9 g)
2. Place sponge guard vein, Danggui, and Clematis in water (1000 mL)
3. Boil for 30 minutes, and save the liquid
4. Add red bean and simmer for 1 hr
5. Add small amount of sugar
6. Eat once a day, seven days in a row

Papaya and Rengdongteng (Casulis Lonicerae) Soup

1. Prepare Green Papaya (500 g), Rengdongteng (30 g), Coix seed (30 g)
2. Clean and put all materials in a pot with water (1500 mL)
3. Put the stove on mid-level heat for one hour.
4. Eat once a day, five days in a row

Chinese Yam and Goji Berry Congee (Good for all types of headache)

1. Prepare rice (100 g), Chinese yam (50 g), berry (30 g)
2. Add rice and Chinese yam to 1000 mL water in a rice cooker
3. When almost done, add goji berry, re-cook five to eight minutes

Bitter Melon (Suitable for Liver Fire headache)

1. Clean and slice bitter melon to half inch thick
2. Stir fry in a pan, cook until soft
3. Season as liked

Tianma (Suitable for Dampness caused headache)

1. Prepare Tianma (80 g), a whole organic chicken, fresh ginger root (8 slices, ¼ inch thick)
2. With water cover chicken, bring to boiling
3. Reduce heat and simmer about 30 minutes
4. Season to taste

Walnut and Sesame Porridge (Good for Kidney Qi weakness headache)

1. Prepare slightly baked walnut (30 g), sesame (30 g), oatmeal (100 g)
2. Grind walnut and sesame into powder

3. Cook oatmeal to porridge and mix well

Longan

100 g dried longan, 2 eggs, appropriate amount of sugar. Mash dried longan, add water to the egg and simmer until the egg is cooked, remove the shell, and simmer for 1 hour. Add sugar. Eat eggs and drink soup.

Congee for Eczema Skin

Put Coix 50 g, red bean 50 g, peanut with red skin 25 g, buckwheat 50 g, millet 100 g into rice cooker, add about 1500-2000 cc water, cook to verging of soft. Serves 4-6.

Congee for Acne Skin

Lily clove 50 g, mung bean 80 g, coix 50 g, millet 150 g, add all the ingredients into rice cooker and about 2000 cc water, cook for half hour. Serves 4-6.

Psoriasis Congee

Astragulus 200 g, Coix 50 g, Chinese yam 30 g, mung bean 50 g, millet 150 g, dry goji berry 30 g. Cook astragulus like the above mentioned method, when congee almost done, add goji berry, simmer for 10 minutes, then it is ready to serve.

Honey Ginger Juice (Suitable for asthma after a cold)

1. Mash 1 ¼ cup ginger to get the juice,
2. Mix ginger with ¼ cup honey
3. Drink with warm water 3 times

White Radish Pepper Soup

Good for people who are depressed and have thick, excessive phlegm that is difficult to cough up.

1. Prepare 1 white radish, 5 white pepper, 4 ginger, and 1 orange peel.
2. Add 2 ¼ cups of water
3. Simmer for 30 minutes
4. Remove the residue and save the liquid
5. Add 1 cup more of water to decoct for 15 minutes
6. Mix well, and refrigerate.
7. Drink twice a day, ½ serving each time, one in the morning and one in the evening.

Almond Grain Rice Tea

Prepare 120 grams of almonds, 30 grams of rice, and 150 grams of sugar. Soak the almonds in boiling water for 15 minutes and soak the rice in cold water for 30 minutes; mix and grind the almonds and rice; add 600 mL of water and sugar and stir while boiling until it becomes a thick juice. It is suitable for patients who carry internal organ pathologies, poor appetite, and cough with white sputum.

Chrysanthemum-Platycodon-Snow Pear Soup

Prepare 5 chamomile, 5 g Platycodon, 1 pear, 5 g rock sugar. Wash the chamomile and Platycodon; add 1200 mL of water and boil; turn to low heat and continue to cook for 10 minutes; remove the residue and leave the juice; add rock sugar, stir well, set aside and let cool. Wash the pears, peel and dice, and add the cold chamomile water. This recipe invigorates lung qi, clears heat and relieves cough. It is suitable for asthma patients with cough, asthma, and yellow sputum.

1. Prepare honeysuckle (1.5 g), dwarf lilyturf (Mai Dong, or Ophiopogon japonicus, 3 g), raw licorice (3 g), and 2 Boat-fruited Scaphium Seeds (Pangdahai, Sterculia lychnophora). Mix in a teacup and prepare as tea. Take 1-2 times daily.

2. Prepare 1 snow pear and 1 Monk Fruit, peel the pear, remove the core, and dice; clean the Monk Fruit, and place with the pear cubes in a pot; add some water, heat to boil, and keep boiling on low heat for 30min. Drink as tea daily. This recipe is good for those with Lung Yin Deficiency.

Japonica Rice, Chicken, Ginger, and Jujube Porridge

Suitable for allergic rhinitis of Wind-Cold type.

Ingredients: 100 g glutinous rice, 5 g ginger, 7 scallions, 10mL of rice vinegar.

Method: Add glutinous rice and ginger and add water to cook the porridge. Add scallions after the porridge is almost cooked. Finally, add rice vinegar.

Ingredients: 10 jujubes (red date), 5 scallions, 100 grams of chicken, 10 grams each of coriander and ginger, 100 grams of japonica rice, and moderate salt.

Method: Boil the japonica rice, chicken, ginger, and jujube. When the porridge is cooked, add salt, white onion, and coriander to taste.

Chrysanthemum and Mulberry Leaves Porridge

Suitable for allergic rhinitis of Wind-Heat type.

Ingredients: 15 grams each of chrysanthemum and mulberry leaves, 60 grams of japonica rice.

Method: Decoct the chrysanthemum and mulberry leaves in water, remove the residue to get the juice, add the japonica rice to the porridge and take it once a day.

Ginger and Walnut Soothing Drink

Suitable for allergic rhinitis of Lung and Kidney yang deficiency.

Ingredients: 3 g ginger, 10 g walnut kernel.
Method: Wash ginger and cut into slices for later use. Put the walnuts in a pot and add 500 mL of water. After boiling for 20 minutes, add the ginger slices and cook for another 5 minutes.
Take once a day.

Chinese Yam Lily Porridge

Nourish Stomach Yin, promote body fluid. It works for Qi deficiency.

Ingredients: 60 grams of yam, 30 grams of lily, 10 jujubes.
Method: Cook the above three flavors in the same pot.

Zhuru Japonica Rice Porridge

To clear away Heat and benefit the Stomach. This recipe works for those with Stomach Heat.

Ingredients: 50 grams of Zhuru, 50 grams of Japonica rice.
Method: Fry Zhuru in water for 15-20 minutes to remove the residue and leave the juice, then add the washed rice and cook it into porridge.

Carrot Rose and Brown Sugar Water

Soothes the Liver and invigorates the Stomach. This recipe works for the people with Liver Qi invading the Stomach.

Ingredients: 250 grams of white radish, 20 grams of roses, appropriate amount of brown sugar.

Method: mash the white radish and roses to make the juice, add brown sugar, and take it with boiling water

Dried Ginger and Tangerine Peel Powder

To warm the Spleen to remove dampness.

Ingredients: 20 grams of dried ginger, 40 grams of tangerine peel, 10-50 grams of brown sugar.

Method: Grind dried ginger and tangerine peel into powder, add brown sugar to water and dissolve until boiling, add the powder, and boil for 5 minutes. Wait it for drying; then, make it into powder. Take 10 grams each time, 3 times a day, with warm water.

Orange Peel Drink

To power the dynamic of Qi and invigorate Spleen.

Ingredients: 60 grams of orange peel

Method: Boil 500 grams of water and orange peel for 2 to 3 minutes. Drink the juice frequently or chew the orange peel.

Banana Water Spinach Porridge

Clear away Heat and detoxification, moisten the intestines, and a laxative.

Ingredients: 100 grams of banana, 100 grams of water spinach (water spinach), 50 grams of japonica rice, cooked together as porridge.

Sophora Japonica Soup

Cool Blood to stop bleeding, remove the Heat.

Ingredients: Sophora japonicus 10 grams, licorice 3 grams
Method: Wash the ingredients together, drain them, put them in a thermos and pour 700cc of boiling water, simmer for 15 minutes, leave to cool and take the soup to drink.

Flower Tea

Enhances Qi and Blood movement.

Ingredients: Rose/3 g, Jasmine /3 g, peony/3 g, safflower/2 g
Method: Make tea with boiled water.

Winter Melon (Wax Gourd) and Rice Soup

Clear away Heat and promote urination.

Ingredients: 350 grams of wax gourd, 50 grams of rice, appropriate amount of sugar.
Method: Wash the wax gourd and cut into pieces. Wash the rice, cook with winter melon into soup, put moderate sugar.

Stewed Duck with American Ginseng

Nourishing Qi and Nourishing Kidney Yin

Ingredients: 5 g of American ginseng, 120 g of teal, 1 piece of ginger

Method: Remove the hair of the teal, cut into pieces, and boil, wash and slice American ginseng, add ginger, add 250 mL of water to the stewing pot, and simmer for two hours. Drink 2 times a day.

Cinnamon Porridge

Warm and tonify Kidney Yang, promote Blood circulation, and urination.

Ingredients: 3 grams of cinnamon, 100 grams of japonica rice, moderate amount of brown sugar.

Method: Cook the cinnamon to make juice, wash the japonica rice and cook the porridge. After the porridge is boiled, add cinnamon juice and brown sugar, and cook until the rice is rotten into porridge.

Shrimp Simmered Lamb

Invigorates the Kidney and Yang. Used for Kidney deficiency and impotence in the elderly.

1. 250 g of lamb, washed and cut into pieces,
2. Add water, and simmered at low heat.
3. When it is mature, add 25 g of shrimp and 5 slices of ginger.
4. Cook until cooked, add a little salt and a little monosodium glutamate,
5. Season to taste.

Ginger and Scallion Root Tea

Remedy for Cold-caused menstrual cramps and stomach ache. It immediately relieves the pain and dissolves mild stagnation, can be used once or twice a day when needed.

Ingredients: 8 slices fresh ginger root, 6 scallion (white part plus roots)

Method: Put both materials in a pot with 800 mL pure water, bring to boil, lower the heat and simmer for 5 minutes, strain the tea into a cup, add brown sugar to taste.

Rose Tea

Has the effects of aromatherapy, relaxes mind and improves the mood, also relieves PMS symptoms and mild pain in lower abdomen. May be used daily, one week before menses.

Ingredients: 10 buds of dried red rose

Method: Boil with 600 mL water, simmer for 5 minutes, then strain the tea into a cup, add organic honey to taste.

Black Bone Chicken and Ginseng Goji Berry Soup

Good for Kidney Liver function weakness, and well known for its therapeutic effects for fatigue, malnutrition, strengthening of Organs and treatment of all deficiencies.

Ingredients: One whole black bone chicken, ginseng 18 g, and goji berry 45 g with pure water 1200ml

Method: Put all materials in a big pot, bring to boil, and simmer for 40 minutes. Seasoning with fresh ginger slices, and green scallion one piece, black pepper and sea salt to taste. This is a tonic food, able to promote Yin Yang balance, boost immunity, and supply the body with natural hormone, great for menopausal individuals with kidney and liver deficiency. Black bone chicken is a delicious nutritionally rich food.

Mung Bean and Rice Porridge

Has the effects of balancing the body and mind. Mung bean is considered the most valuable due to its ability to purge toxins from the body, and help reach a goal of losing weight.

Ingredients: One cup of each ingredient

Method: Add 8 cups water in pot, bring to boil, lower heat, simmer for half hour. Rice may be replaced by buckwheat, millet or barley.

Pearl Barley and Brown Rice Porridge

Suitable for individuals with weak Spleen.

Ingredients: One cup each of pearl barley and brown rice.

Method: Soak before cooking for one hour, then drain off the water, put in pot, add 8 cups water, bring to boil, lower heat to simmer for about one hour or until soft.

Tomato and Vegetable Soup

Good for people with blood sugar imbalance, able to quench craving, easily lose 10 pounds in a few weeks.

Method: Use tomato as the largest portion, add equal portion of onion, carrot, celery, and cabbage, pure water and some herbs such as ginger, rosemary or thyme. Black pepper, cayenne pepper, put in slow-cooker for one hour. It is better to eat this for 5-7 days, eat as much as you like. A couple in their 70s who are both overweight and with slightly higher than normal blood glucose levels consumed this soup for two weeks and each lost about 10 pounds.

Barley Water

Barley is highly nutritious, good for digestion, decongests the chest and expels dampness.

Ingredients: Barley 30 g, pure water 1L.

Method: Place in a stove pot, bring to boil, and simmer for about one hour, strain into cup and drink hot.

White Fungus and Black Fungus Soup

Clear away Heat to moisten Lung, and nourish Kidney, and nourish Yin.

Ingredients: 10 grams each of white fungus and black fungus.

Method: Soak the black and white fungus in warm water, remove the stalks and impurities, wash and place in a container, add an appropriate amount of water, and steam for 1 hour. Eat fungus and drink soup. Take once a day.

Goji and Egg Crepes

Nourish the Kidney and nourish Yin, benefit Essence, and improve eyesight.

Ingredients: 10 grams of Chinese wolfberry, 2 eggs.

Method: Put the unshelled eggs into a bowl, add the washed goji and an appropriate amount of water, stir vigorously, and steam the food over water. Use once a day for 10-15 days.

Ginseng and Asparagus Congee

Nourish Yin and Replenish Qi.

Ingredients: 6 g of ginseng, 30 g of asparagus, 100 g of japonica rice.

Method: Cut ginseng and asparagus into thin slices, put in water and cook for 20 minutes, then add japonica rice to make porridge. Drink 1 bowl each morning and evening, and take it for 7-10 days.

Fresh Milk Walnut Paste

Replenish the Spleen and Kidney, warm Yang and nourish Yin.

Ingredients: 1000 g milk, 40 g fried walnut meat, 20 g raw walnut meat, 50 g japonica rice.

Method: Wash the japonica rice, soak it in water for 1 hour, remove and drain the water. Put the four things together and stir them evenly, grind them with a powerful blender. Add water to a pot and boil, slowly pour the milk walnut paste into the pot, stir while pouring, and serve. Take it for 3 to 4 weeks.

Herbal Tea

Both cassia seed and goji berry are known for their activity in putting off the Liver fire, and goji berry is also a tonifying agent that helps with Liver, Kidney, and Spleen deficiencies.

Ingredients: 50 grams of Cassia Seed, 15 grams of Goji berries, and 30 grams of Rock Sugar.

Method: Stir-fry the cassia seeds for a while, mash them, put them in a teapot together with Goji berries and rock sugar, pour an appropriate amount of boiling water, cover and suffocate for 15 minutes, drink frequently instead of tea, 1 dose per day. Cassia Seed available on Amazon.

Note: the addition of rock sugar in this recipe can not only improve the taste, but also nourish the Yin and promote the body fluid. However, it should be noted that people with diabetes are not suitable to use rock candy, they can simply use goji berries and cassia seed to make tea.

Chinese Yam, Goji Berry and Chicken Soup

Chinese yam is tonic to Spleen and Kidney, and goji berry tonic to Liver and Kidney, both nourish the brain and replenish Qi and Blood. Shiitake mushroom is delicious with rich nutrients that enhance immunity and prevent diseases.

Ingredients: One organic whole chicken, 10 shiitake mushrooms, goji berry and Chinese yam 30 g each, one cup rice wine, sea salt, ginger, pepper and green onion.

Method: Put all materials and chicken into a pot, except green onion, add water to cover chicken, and bring to boil, lower heat, cover pot, and simmer for 40 minutes. Sprinkle some sea salt, pepper, and minced green onion. Serves 8-10.

Pollen and Honey Tea

A natural remedy for healing and preventing diseases, and provides potent sources of essential fatty acids, amino acids, and trace elements.

Ingredients: 2 tsp bee pollen, 1 tsp honey.

Method: Put into a large mug, then fill mug with very warm (not boiling) water 500ml, stir well and drink immediately. Pollen can be replaced with 1 tsp royal jelly.

Ginseng Sanqi Tea

Tonifies energy, unblocks Blood stasis, and is helpful for AD and vascular dementia sufferers.

Ingredients: Ginseng (Panax ginseng) 5 g, Sanqi (Panax notoginseng) 5 g (both sliced)

Method: Put into a mug, add boiling water, cover and steep for 10 minutes. Mug may be refilled up with warm water a few times throughout the day. This herbal elixir may be used on a daily basis.

Eight Treasure Tea

Ingredients: 50 g black rice, 50 g glutinous rice, 30 g barley, 30 g kidney bean, 30 g red bean, 30 g mung bean, 5 Chinese dates, 10 lotus seeds, 15 peanuts, 5 longans

Method: Put into a mug, add around 1000 mL boiling water, cover and steep for 10 minutes. Mug may be refilled up with warm water a few times throughout the day. This herbal amount of each ingredient may be adjusted by personal choice.

FINDING THE RIGHT TCM THERAPIST

Now you have insight into some of the concepts of TCM, you and your ever-flowing Qi may want to explore even more options. It's exciting to know TCM doctors and specialists have unique, complementary methods for healing and optimizing health—namely in the form of acupuncture or herbal formulas specially designed for your needs. (One of the reasons we don't discuss acupuncture in-depth is because it needs to be performed by a specialist—no self-needling please!).

Navigating any new area of health can feel like you're trekking into a midnight-black cave with no map and no light. That's why it's helpful to have some guidance. Here are some important things to consider when finding the Chinese medicine practitioner or acupuncturist that's right for you*:

CHECK OUT REGISTRATION AND TITLES

Always find a practitioner who is registered or licensed to practice in your area. Pay attention to the registration titles of the therapist based on your needs.

IN THE U.S.

The National Certification Commission for Acupuncture and Oriental Medicine (NCCAOM) website has a national directory of all acupuncturists and TCM practitioners that hold NCCAOM certification. Currently, 47 states, plus the District of Columbia, require NCCAOM certification or the passing of NCCAOM examinations as a prerequisite for licensure to practice acupuncture. Each state board has a unique set of licensing requirements.

Diplomate of Acupuncture: Specializes in acupuncture only.

Diplomate of Oriental Medicine: Specializes in both acupuncture and Chinese herbal medicine.

IN CANADA

Registered Acupuncturist (R.Ac.): A registrant authorized to practice acupuncture.

Registered Traditional Chinese Medicine Practitioner (R.TCM.P.): A registrant authorized to practice acupuncture and prescribe, compound, or dispense Chinese herbal medicine.

GET REFERRALS

You do it for plumbers, carpet cleaners, dog groomers, dentists, doctors, restaurants…just about anything. Do the same when it comes to TCM practitioners. Find someone you trust to vouch for their quality of knowledge and service.

Ask your primary care doctor for a referral list of acupuncturists or ask other health care providers for recommendations. Talk to family and friends who have received TCM treatment about who they'd recommend. Some online resources will rank different clinics in your area, but please note there is currently no authoritative organization in North America that ranks Chinese medicine clinics. Although all TCM clinics can provide general treatment for most illnesses and conditions, some may specialize in particular areas, such as infertility. This is something you can ask as you're reaching out to explore clinics close to you.

Yes, you'll want to consider location. Most chronic diseases will require multiple acupuncture and Chinese medicine treatments over time, and you'll want a consultation before starting any treatment. Finding a practitioner closer to home will make the process easier.

FIND THE RIGHT FIT

TCM emphasizes the relationship between the body and mind. It's always best to have a good relationship with your doctor—one that feels like a good fit between the two of you (there's that Yin and Yang again!). How will you know?

You should feel extremely comfortable talking to your chosen provider. And they should welcome your questions and answer them in a way you can easily understand. Remember, you can always stop a consultation or treatment at any time if you don't feel comfortable. In addition, during your consultation your provider should show an interest in your current condition and your overall health history using "Diagnoses by asking." Afterall, it's one of the four key methods used to determine your Chinese medicine diagnoses (see Assessment on page 65). These are often "When and What" questions and may differ from those you're typically asked by a Western doctor.

Note: Alberta, Quebec, and Newfoundland and Labrador regulate acupuncturists only. There are two additional registration titles in British Columbia: Traditional Chinese Medicine Herbalist (R.TCM.H.) *and* Doctor of Traditional Chinese Medicine (Dr.TCM). *You can refer to the College of Traditional Chinese Medicine Practitioners + Acupuncturists of British Columbia for more information.*

THE 5 ELEMENT CHEAT SHEET

Element	Wood	Fire	Earth	Metal	Water
Primary Organ	Liver	Heart	Spleen	Lungs	Kidneys
Paired Organ	Gallbladder	Small Intestine	Stomach	Large Intestine	Urinary Bladder
Emotion	Anger	Joy	Worry	Grief	Fear
Color	Cyan	Red	Yellow	White	Black
Taste	Sour	Bitter	Sweet	Pungent	Salty
Season	Spring	Summer	Late Summer	Fall	Winter
Energy	Wind	Heat	Dampness	Dryness	Cold
Sensory Organ and Sense	Eyes/Vision	Tongue/Speech	Mouth/Taste	Nose/Smell	Ears/Hearing
Related Organs	Tendons, Ligaments	Pulse, Veins, Arteries	Muscles, Flesh	Skin	Bones, Joints
External Manifestation	Nails	Facial Complexion	Lips	Body Hair	Head Hair
Body Fluid	Tears	Sweat	Saliva	Mucus	Urine
Phonetics	Mi	So	Do	Re	La
Abstract Function	Generating	Governing	Transforming	Harvesting	Conserving
Physiological Functions	Digestion, Qi Movement, Menstruation, Sleep, Store Blood	Blood Vessels, Circulation	Immune System, Digestion, Absorption, Metabolism, Blood, Containment	Breathing, Water Passage	Growth, Development, Reproduction, Sexual Function
Spiritual and Mental Function	Hun (the Ethereal Soul), Vision, Decision Making, Strategy, Judgment	Shen (the Emperor of the Soul), Consciousness, Perception, Cognition, Emotion, Language, Initiative	Yi (the Mindful Soul), Thoughts, Ideas, Intention, Reasoning	Po (the Corporal Soul), Mental Discipline, Order, Sensitivity, Restraint	Zhi (the Willful Soul), Motivation, Determination, Willpower, Coordination
Mental Quality	Sensitivity	Creativity	Clarity	Intuition	Spontaneity
Sound	Shouting	Laughing	Singing	Weeping	Moaning

Smell	Rancid or Foul	Burnt	Sweet or Fragrant	Rank or Fishy	Putrid
Sign of Illness	Exhibiting Logorrhea	Belching	Slurring	Coughing	Yawning
Grains and Vegetables	Wheat, Mallow	Beans, Greens	Rice, Scallions	Corn, Onions	Millet, Leeks

ACKNOWLEDGMENTS

This book has been a microcosm of the Yin-Yang philosophy and the idea of Qi. Our team—all with different strengths—brought balance and energy to the whole process. It was a true team effort. One that was both difficult and fun, as we wanted to create a vision for how to better bridge medical approaches between the East and West.

To make it possible, we have to thank the team at USANA, especially Dr. Robert Sinnott, Dr. Jeremy Tian, Dr. Rolando Maddela, and Emma Davenport. They all made important and valuable contributions to the book. Special thanks to Dr. Tian, whose experience in both Western and Eastern medicine made him *Yin Yang You's* life force. More thanks to Cindy Yearley for expert and spot-on editing, Willow Withy for her design concepts, and instrumental team members Sean Derber, DiChen McCoy, and Dan Macuga, who all worked tirelessly behind the scenes to make it happen.

This book revisits the fundamentals of TCM which required the wonderful support of our superb consultants Jun Jimmy Wang, Jianping Jenny Shi, and Junrong John Wu.

Thank you to Nadia Chen for her stunning illustrations that artistically captured the spirit of TCM and to Ted Spiker for writing that aimed to make the conversation about TCM clear and compelling—with a dash of fun.

Anlong Xu appreciates the wonderful support from the entire Beijing University of Chinese Medicine faculty and staff who have built the world-class clinical, educational, and research institution that informs the pages of this book. TCM expert Dr. Lepeng Wang elegantly described TCM practice to make this beautiful process accessible for a Western audience. Other team members include Dr. Minke Tang and Dr. Kay Yuan who have contributed their TCM international experience and expertise. Special thanks to research team members Dr. Guangrui Huang, Dr. Jianhua Zhen, Dr. Wenrui Jia, Dr. Yuxiu Sun, and Dr. Pengfei Zhao for their assistance.

Mehmet Oz especially thanks his colleagues at NY Presbyterian-Columbia University, The Dr Oz Show, and USANA, who all share a deep passion for improving the world's health. Collectively, they have supported efforts to bring traditional healing approaches from many countries together so we can all share these ancient teachings.